**SEMINAR STUDIES** IN HISTORY

# The Origins of the Vietnam War

FREDRIK LOGEVALL

*An imprint of* **Pearson Education**

Harlow, England · London · New York · Reading, Massachusetts · San Francisco · Toronto · Don Mills, Ontario · Sydney
Tokyo · Singapore · Hong Kong · Seoul · Taipei · Cape Town · Madrid · Mexico City · Amsterdam · Munich · Paris · Milan

**Pearson Education Limited**
Edinburgh Gate
Harlow
Essex CM20 2JE
England
*and Associated Companies throughout the world.*

*Visit us on the World Wide Web at:*
www.pearsoned.co.uk

First published 2001

ISBN 978-0-582-31918-9

**British Library Cataloguing-in-Publication Data**
A catalogue record for this book is
available from the British Library

**Library of Congress Cataloging-in-Publication Data**
Logevall, Fredrik, 1963–
    The origins of the Vietnam War / Fredrik Logevall.
      p. cm. -- (Seminar studies in history)
    Includes bibliographical references and index.
    ISBN 0-582-31918-8 (alk. paper)
      1. Vietnamese Conflict, 1961–1975. 2. Vietnam--History--1945–1975. I. Title.
    II. Series.

DS557.6 .L64 2001
959.704′3--dc21                                                    2001029311

11   10
10   09   08

Set by 7 in 10/12 Sabon Roman
Printed in Malaysia, LSP

The Origins of the Vietnam War

Pearson
Education

We work with leading authors to develop the
strongest educational materials in history,
bringing cutting-edge thinking and best learning
practice to a global market.

Under a range of well-known imprints, including
Longman, we craft high-quality print and electronic
publications which help readers to understand and
apply their content, whether studying or at work.

To find out more about the complete range of our
publishing please visit us on the World Wide Web at:
www.pearsoneduc.com

# CONTENTS

# INTRODUCTION TO THE SERIES

Such is the pace of historical enquiry in the modern world that there is an ever-widening gap between the specialist article or monograph, incorporating the results of current research, and general surveys, which inevitably become out of date. *Seminar Studies in History* is designed to bridge this gap. The series was founded by Patrick Richardson in 1966 and his aim was to cover major themes in British, European and world history. Between 1980 and 1996 Roger Lockyer continued his work, before handing the editorship over to Clive Emsley and Gordon Martel. Clive Emsley is Professor of History at the Open University, while Gordon Martel is Professor of International History at the University of Northern British Columbia, Canada, and Senior Research Fellow at De Montfort University.

All the books are written by experts in their field who are not only familiar with the latest research but have often contributed to it. They are frequently revised, in order to take account of new information and interpretations. They provide a selection of documents to illustrate major themes and provoke discussion, and also a guide to further reading. The aim of *Seminar Studies in History* is to clarify complex issues without over-simplifying them, and to stimulate readers into deepening their knowledge and understanding of major themes and topics.

# NOTE ON REFERENCING SYSTEM

Readers should note that numbers in square brackets [5] refer them to the corresponding entry in the Bibliography at the end of the book (specific page numbers are given in italics). A number in square brackets preceded by *Doc*. [*Doc. 5*] refers readers to the corresponding item in the Documents section which follows the main text.

# ACKNOWLEDGEMENTS

We are grateful to the following for permission to reproduce copyright material:

Lyndon Baines Johnson Library and Museum for an extract by President Lyndon B Johnson in *Public Papers of the Presidents of the United States: Lyndon B Johnson*, 1965, Government Printing Office, Washington, DC, pp. 394–7; The Kennedy Library for an extract from Box 301 National Security Files, Vietnam Country Series, Memos and Miscellaneous, Confidential, 1 November 1961; The New York Times for an extract from the article 'Pham Van Dong ... on Viet Nam' in the *New York Times* 14/4/1965; Gareth Porter for an extract translated from Le Duan, the General Secretary of the Vietnamese Workers' Party and the editor, Gareth Porter, for the translation of an extract from Ho Chi Min letter dated 22/10/1945 in *Vietnam: The Definitive Documentation of Human Decisions*, 2 vols, edited by Gareth Porter, 1949; US Department of State for extracts from 'Taylor Papers' T–157–69 30/12/1964, National Defense University and Humphrey Memorandum, Washington, February 17, 1965, Minnesota History Society, Hubert H Humphrey Papers – Vietnam 1965–1968.

# LIST OF ABBREVIATIONS

| | |
|---|---|
| ARVN | Army of the Republic of Vietnam |
| CIA | Central Intelligence Agency |
| DMZ | Demilitarized Zone |
| DRV | Democratic Republic of Vietnam (North Vietnam) |
| EDC | European Defense Community |
| FDR | Franklin D. Roosevelt |
| ICC | International Commission on Supervision and Control |
| ICP | Indochinese Communist Party |
| JCS | Joint Chiefs of Staff |
| JFK | John F. Kennedy |
| LBJ | Lyndon B. Johnson |
| MACV | Military Assistance Command, Vietnam |
| NATO | North Atlantic Treaty Organization |
| NLF | National Front for the Liberation of Vietnam |
| NSC | National Security Council |
| OPLAN | Operations Plan |
| PAVN | People's Army of Vietnam (North Vietnam) |
| RVN | Republic of Vietnam (South Vietnam) |
| SEATO | Southeast Asia Treaty Organization |
| UN | United Nations |
| VNQDD | Vietnamese Nationalist Party |

*Map 1* French Indochina

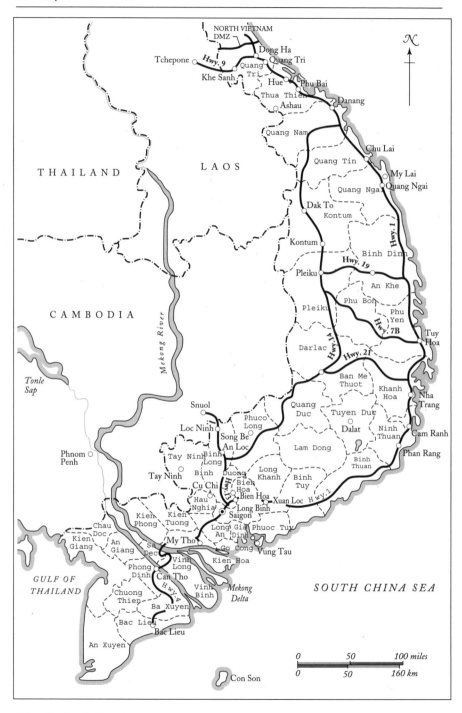

*Map 2*  South Vietnam

*Map 3.* Vietnam and Southeast Asian Mainland, 1954–75

# CHRONOLOGY

| | |
|---|---|
| *1884* | France solidifies its control of Vietnam, establishing a 'protectorate' over Annam and Tonkin and ruling Cochin China as a colony. |
| *1890* | Ho Chi Minh born in central Vietnam. |
| *1911* | Ho departs from Vietnam, not to return for thirty years. |
| *1920* | Ho joins the newly formed French Communist Party. |
| *1930* | Ho and colleagues form the Indochinese Communist Party. |
| *1939* | World War II breaks out in Europe as Germany invades Poland. |
| *1940* | |
| June | France falls to the Germans. |
| September | Japan takes Indochina but leaves the French colonial administration intact. |
| *1941* | |
| June | Ho Chi Minh returns to Vietnam, and forms the Vietminh. |
| *1945* | |
| 9 March | Japan deposes the French puppet government in Vietnam and assumes control. |
| 12 April | Franklin D. Roosevelt dies; Harry S. Truman becomes president of the United States. |
| 8 May | Germany surrenders. |
| 15 August | Japan capitulates, after the United States drops atomic bombs on Hiroshima and Nagasaki, and after the USSR enters the war. |
| 29 August | Ho Chi Minh proclaims provisional government in Hanoi. |
| 2 September | Ho declares Vietnam independent. |
| *1946* | |
| May | Ho travels to France for negotiations. |
| September | Negotiations break down, though a meaningless *modus vivendi* is signed. Ho leaves Paris. |

| | |
|---|---|
| November | Warfare breaks out in Vietnam. |
| 19 December | General Vo Nguyen Giap declares a war of national resistance. |

### 1949

| | |
|---|---|
| 8 March | Bao Dai signs agreement making Vietnam an 'associated state' within the French Union. |
| 19 July | Laos becomes an 'associated state' within the French Union. |
| 1 October | Mao Zedong proclaims the establishment of the People's Republic of China. |
| 8 November | Cambodia becomes an 'associated state' within the French Union. |

### 1950

| | |
|---|---|
| June | Korean War begins. |
| 26 July | Truman signs legislation granting military aid to the French for the war in Indochina. |
| 6 December | General Jean de Lattre de Tassigny named French military commander and high commissioner for Indochina. |

### 1951

| | |
|---|---|
| February | Vietnamese Workers' Party (Lao Dong) formed. |

### 1952

| | |
|---|---|
| 11 January | De Lattre dies in Paris. |

### 1954

| | |
|---|---|
| 13 March | Battle of Dien Bien Phu begins. |
| 5 April | US President Dwight D. Eisenhower voices public concern about 'falling dominoes'. |
| 7 May | French defeated at Dien Bien Phu. |
| 8 May | Indochina phase of Geneva Conference opens, with Great Britain and the Soviet Union as co-chairmen. |
| 16 June | Bao Dai selects Ngo Dinh Diem as prime minister. |
| July | Geneva Accords signed. |
| 8 September | Southeast Asia Treaty Organization (SEATO) formed, by the United States, Britain, France, Australia, New Zealand, Pakistan, Thailand, and the Philippines. |

**1955**

January       United States begins to funnel aid directly to the Saigon government, and agrees to train South Vietnamese army.

23 October       Diem defeats Bao Dai in a referendum.

December       Land reform in North Vietnam reaches its most radical phase.

**1956**

August       Ho Chi Minh apologizes for the excesses of the Agricultural Reform Tribunals.

**1957**

8 May       Diem arrives for ten-day visit to the United States.

**1959**

Spring       Insurgency in South Vietnam gains momentum. North Vietnam forms Group 559, to begin infiltrating men and weapons into the South.

**1960**

20 December       National Front for the Liberation of South Vietnam (NLF) formed.

**1961**

January       As he leaves office, Eisenhower warns John F. Kennedy that Laos is the key to holding the line in Southeast Asia.

May       Vice-President Lyndon Johnson visits South Vietnam.

16 May       Geneva Conference on Laos opens.

October       Maxwell Taylor and Walt W. Rostow visit South Vietnam.

**1962**

6 February       Military Assistance Command Vietnam (MACV) formed.

23 July       Geneva Agreement creates 'neutral and independent' Laos, with a coalition government headed by Souvanna Phouma.

August       US military advisers in South Vietnam have grown from 700 to 12,000.

**1963**

2 January       Vietcong units defeat the South Vietnamese at the battle of Ap Bac.

| | |
|---|---|
| 8 May | South Vietnamese troops and police fire on Buddhist demonstrators in Hué. |
| 29 August | French President Charles de Gaulle calls for Vietnam to be free of outside interference. |
| 1 November | Diem overthrown in coup led by Duong Van Minh. |
| 2 November | Diem and his brother, Ngo Dinh Nhu, assassinated. |
| 22 November | John F. Kennedy murdered in Dallas; succeeded by Lyndon B. Johnson. |
| December | Ninth Plenum of the Vietnamese Workers' Party. |

*1964*

| | |
|---|---|
| January | France extends diplomatic recognition to the People's Republic of China. |
| 16 January | Johnson initiates OPLAN 34-A. |
| 30 January | General Nguyen overthrows Minh junta and seizes power in Saigon. |
| April | State Department launches 'More Flags' campaign, to get increased international support for South Vietnam. |
| June | Canadian diplomat J. Blair Seaborn visits Hanoi. |
| 2 August | North Vietnamese patrol boats attack the *Maddox*, an American destroyer in the Gulf of Tonkin. A doubtful second attack is reported two days later. |
| 7 August | Congress passes the Gulf of Tonkin resolution, giving Johnson broad power to act in Southeast Asia. |
| 3 November | Johnson wins landslide election victory over Barry Goldwater. NSC Working Group meets for the first time to discuss US strategy. |
| 1 December | Johnson administration opts to implement a two-phase escalation aimed at turning the conflict around. |
| 30 December | Lyndon Johnson cables Ambassador Taylor in Saigon and says he is prepared to increase substantially the number of American forces in South Vietnam. |

*1965*

| | |
|---|---|
| 4 February | National Security Adviser McGeorge Bundy arrives in Saigon, and Soviet Prime Minister Aleksei Kosygin visits Hanoi. |
| 7 February | Vietcong stage attacks against US installation at Pleiku. Johnson authorizes Flaming Dart, American air raids against North Vietnam. |
| 10 February | Vietcong attack American barracks at Qui Nhon, and Johnson again orders retaliation. |

| | |
|---|---|
| 2 March | United States commences Rolling Thunder, sustained bombing on North Vietnam. |
| 8 March | Two Marine battalions land near Danang, the first American combat troops in Vietnam. |
| 7 April | LBJ, at Johns Hopkins University, gives widely publicized speech in which he appears to leave the door open to diplomacy. |
| 8 April | Prime Minister Pham Van Dong responds to Johnson's call by issuing a four-point basis for peace. |
| May | By mid-month, 47,000 US ground troops are in South Vietnam. |
| 11 June | Air Vice-Marshal Nguyen Cao Ky takes over as prime minister of a military regime in Saigon. |
| 28 July | Johnson approves General William Westmoreland's request for forty-four additional combat batallions. |
| December | American troop strength in Vietnam reaches close to 200,000. |

*1973*

| | |
|---|---|
| 23 January | Paris Peace Agreement signed. |
| 29 March | Last American troops leave Vietnam. |

*1975*

| | |
|---|---|
| 30 April | South Vietnamese government surrenders. |

# CHAPTER ONE

# INTRODUCTION: THE PROBLEM

At two o'clock in the morning on 7 February 1965, shortly after the end of a cease-fire to mark the Tet holiday, a company of Vietcong guerrillas launched an attack on a loosely guarded US helicopter base and barracks near Pleiku in the Central Highlands of South Vietnam. Eight Americans were killed, 126 wounded, and ten US aircraft destroyed. It was one of about a dozen attacks on targets throughout South Vietnam launched by the Vietcong on this day, and it produced the highest number of American casualties of any incident in the conflict thus far. In Saigon, the US national security adviser, McGeorge Bundy, who was about to complete a three-day visit to South Vietnam, called the White House on a secure telephone line and recommended the prompt initiation of reprisal air strikes against North Vietnam.

In Washington it was still the evening of 6 February when Bundy's call came in. Within hours, President Lyndon Baines Johnson (LBJ) convened the National Security Council (NSC) and secured near-unanimous assent for attacks on four pre-selected targets in southern North Vietnam, to be carried out by 132 US and 22 South Vietnamese planes. The South Vietnamese government was never consulted about the decision. The intensity of Johnson's feelings can be seen in his actions in the intervening hours. He retired to bed at midnight but awoke to talk on the phone with the Defense Department's Cyrus Vance, presumably about the results of the air strikes, at 3.40, 4.10, 4.55, and 5.10 in the morning, finally rising at 6.45.

These were not the first American attacks on North Vietnam. Six months earlier, following a clash between US and North Vietnamese ships in the Gulf of Tonkin off the Northern coast, LBJ had ordered a one-time retaliatory strike. This time, however, the air raid would be no isolated incident. For in the weeks leading up to McGeorge Bundy's visit to South Vietnam, American officials had made the decision to escalate the war in Vietnam, to increase dramatically the level of American involvement in the effort to defeat the Vietcong and end the insurgency. They had opted, in essence, to take over the war from their South Vietnamese allies (though the latter would continue to play a significant role in the fighting), and they entered the month of February seeking an opportunity to initiate the new policy. Pleiku, it is clear, represented a pretext more than a cause.

On 10 February, therefore, Lyndon Johnson ordered another major retaliatory strike, this time in response to a Vietcong attack on American barracks at Qui Nhon, 75 miles east of Pleiku on the central coast. (Guerrillas had planted a 100lb bomb under a building, and the ensuing blast killed 23 American servicemen.) Three days after that, the administration formally agreed to initiate regular, sustained bombing of North Vietnam *and* enemy-held areas of South Vietnam. On the 19th, US planes attacked enemy-held areas of South Vietnam. On the 19th, US planes bombed various parts of Bindinh province in the South, the first air attack on Vietcong forces in which no South Vietnamese airmen were involved. The assault, carried out by waves of F-100s and B-57s, would last a week and would be expanded to targets throughout the South. On the 26th, the White House agreed to the request of General William Westmoreland, commander of American forces in the war, for two battalions of Marines to guard the air base at Danang, thus introducing the first US ground troops to the war. The decision came after minimal discussion and over Saigon ambassador Maxwell Taylor's objections, and neither Congress nor the South Vietnamese leadership was consulted in advance. On 2 March, six days before the Marines would come ashore, more than one hundred American planes hit targets inside North Vietnam. It was the first attack carried out not in retaliation, and it marked the start of Operation Rolling Thunder [31].

It also marked the cross-over point to major war. The level of fighting increased dramatically, and the chances for early negotiations leading to a negotiated settlement diminished. In the spring and summer months more American ground troops arrived, and the Hanoi government, girding itself for a long struggle, increased its infiltration of men and matériel to the South. By the end of 1965, 180,000 US ground forces were in South Vietnam, and the number would grow until in 1968 it reached over half a million. Hanoi matched each American escalation with one of its own. By the time a settlement was finally reached, at the beginning of 1973, under terms no better than Washington could have had in 1964, or 1965, or 1969, 58,000 Americans and between three and four million Vietnamese lay dead, and much of Vietnam and neighboring Laos and Cambodia lay in ruins.

How to explain the origins of this war is a question that has animated scholars, journalists, and other authors since practically the moment the fighting began. Some have endorsed the position articulated by US officials at the time, that Washington fought in order to defend an ally suffering from external aggression, and that major war happened because Hanoi would not relinquish its drive to take South Vietnam by force. Others have emphasized the role of America's larger strategic considerations, specifically concerns that US credibility would suffer a grievous blow if Vietnam were 'lost' – Washington's allies would henceforth be unable to depend on her for their protection, and communist governments would be emboldened to challenge American power all over the globe. The 'credibility' explanation won favor from many former US officials, who would often combine it with the 'help a friend' argument in explaining the reasons for intervention [106; 161].

These official and semi-official explanations for the war have failed to impress some authors, who have consequently directed their attention elsewhere. For some, the keys to understanding the war lie not in Vietnam or in the international system but in the United States. The fallout from the 'loss of China' and the pressure this put on Democrats in particular always to appear tough on communism; the lingering effects of McCarthyism and the chill this sent down the spine of American leaders; the ostensibly powerful 'Cold War Consensus' in American domestic opinion, which, so the argument goes, led virtually all elite voices in US society to favor a staunch commitment to South Vietnam – all these have been cited to explain the decision for war. Some who emphasize domestic American causes focus on long-term, impersonal, structural reasons for intervention; others stress the short-term, individual, and contingent ones. Some point to the large foreign policy bureaucracy in Washington as being ultimately responsible, as framing the range of choices open to policy-makers and ultimately dictating the policy choice; others give primacy to the president and his closest advisers.

Still others have put forth interpretations that emphasize the role played by American economic imperatives. The most sophisticated exponents of the neo-colonialist model avoid crude economic determinism in their analysis. They acknowledge that Vietnam itself was not economically valuable to the United States and instead make a much broader argument: that policy-makers sought, as one author has put it, 'to create an integrated, essentially capitalist world framework out of the chaos of World War Two and the remnants of the colonial systems' [112 *p. 72*]. Vietnam became important because the revolution there – a leftist, nationalistic revolution – posed a threat to this global capitalist system. Should that revolution be allowed to succeed, other revolutionaries the world over could get inspired; hence the need to try to stop it.

Disparate though these explanations often are, they share one thing in common: virtually all are fundamentally America-centric in explaining the developments that over a period of two decades would lead to war. On one level, the present volume is no different. Any satisfactory history of the origins of the war has to be American-centered to some degree – as informed observers around the world understood, the expansion or resolution of the conflict depended to an inordinate degree on decisions made in Washington. At the same time, however, I aim to place US decision-making in its wider international context. To reach the fullest under-standing of the origins of the war it is essential to bring US leaders' foreign counterparts into the equation, to consider how these leaders approached the Vietnam issue and how their policies influenced, or did not influence, Washington's thinking. This includes not only – and most obviously – the Vietnamese leaders, both northern and southern, but also officials in other major capitals around the world, in Moscow and Beijing, Paris and London, Ottawa and Tokyo. Only by placing American policy in this wider context can we hope to understand the sources and consequences of US officials' decisions, the choices they faced, the options they did or did not have. Employing this wider lens is also essential if we are to understand why diplomacy could not stop the outbreak of major war [121].

What is more, a more international approach to the question is now more possible than it used to be, due to the release of important new information from archives the world over, as well as the declassification of hundreds of hours of taped White House conversations from the Kennedy and Johnson years [13; 213]. The time is right, in short, to look afresh at the making of the tragedy that was the Vietnam War. And because the roots of the war were deep, it is necessary to begin earlier, at a time when another Western power sought to impose its will on Vietnam.

# PART ONE    THE BACKGROUND

# CHAPTER TWO

# THE FRANCO-VIETMINH WAR

## THE COMING OF THE FRENCH

For much of their history, the Vietnamese people have struggled against foreign invaders. Their traditional enemy was China, which dominated Vietnam for more than a thousand years. In reaction, the Vietnamese long ago developed a warrior tradition and a strong sense of national identity. In the fifteenth century, having gained their autonomy from China, the Vietnamese started to expand southward, eventually gaining control of the fertile Mekong Delta, until then a part of Cambodia. By 1802, with the establishment of the Nguyen dynasty, they occupied virtually all the territory that is Vietnam today.

In the decades that followed, however, Vietnam was torn by civil strife between rival claimants to power. In one of these internal conflicts, the leader of a southern-based faction unified the country with the help of French mercenaries. His reliance on France opened the way to steadily increasing French involvement in the country. In 1850, under the pretext of protecting Vietnamese Catholics – French missionary work having introduced Catholicism centuries earlier – France began its conquest of the country. By 1884, Vietnam had come under French colonial domination [24; 118].

The Paris government also established control over neighboring Cambodia and Laos, and by the turn of the century all three acquisitions were formally organized into the French Indochinese Union, to be governed by a governor-general appointed by Paris. After 1893, French Indochina was made up of five administrative departments: Cochin China, a colony in southern Vietnam, and the four protectorates of Cambodia, Laos, Annam (central Vietnam), and Tonkin (northern Vietnam).

Various objectives motivated French colonial policy in Indochina. Some elites argued that the other European powers, including even little Belgium, were outpacing France overseas, and that it was vital to do something, lest French power and prestige slip further. More specifically, the acquisition of Indochina would allow France to compete with the British, who had established a vast colonial empire in Asia stretching from India to the eastern half of New Guinea. The French military establishment, humiliated in France's defeat by Prussia in 1870, relished the opportunity to salve its wounded pride through a fresh foreign enterprise, while bankers and manufacturers sought to exploit the natural resources of Indochina and open up new markets for French goods. For many government officials, these aims were mutually reinforcing and only proved the case for intervention.

The policy was not without critics in France. Humanitarians argued that an imperial policy would bring much misery and little benefit to the Indochinese people, while other opponents maintained that the nation's resources were being drained on behalf of a dubious prize; far better, they thought, to give priority to strengthening France's position in Europe. In the main, however, the French public backed the colonial venture in Indochina, in part because leaders proved skillful in emphasizing the moral aspect of colonialism. That is, they spoke in terms of the so-called civilizing mission (*mission civilisatrice*) – the obligation of the advanced peoples of the world to bring the benefits of advanced Western civilization to the primitive peoples of Asia and Africa. The 'white man's burden,' Rudyard Kipling had called it. In Indochina, so the argument went, France would not only bring economic development but create a modern society based on representative government, the rule of law, and individual freedom.

Of course, it was one thing to proclaim the existence of a French civilizing mission, and another to know how to carry it out. To what degree should the Indochinese be encouraged to embrace the full range of French values and institutions? Should they be allowed to retain indigenous concepts? Were Asian people necessarily destined to repeat the path to industrial development and democracy now being trod in the West? Or were the differences between East and West too great ever to be overcome?

Very soon, it became clear that there were in fact serious contradictions between the publicized goal of the civilizing mission and the more pragmatic objective of exploiting the resources of the colonial territories for the benefit of the home country. Determined to preserve Indochina as a market for manufactured goods produced in their own factories, the French discouraged the emergence of an indigenous industrial and commercial sector that could compete with French imports. They also showed scant interest in encouraging the development of political institutions that could reflect the aspirations of the Indochinese people. The reason was obvious: the French knew only too well that the establishment of popular legislative assemblies would lead to pressure for greater autonomy and, ultimately, the restoration of independence. From the beginning, French colonial policy was marked by ambivalence, and a coherent statement of political and social objectives in Indochina never materialized.

Just why France chose to divide Vietnam into three separate regions is not altogether clear. Partly, no doubt, it was an attempt at the historic imperial tactic of 'divide and rule,' and partly officials hoped it would make the task of administration easier. Regardless, the decision would shape the future of French rule in the region in crucial ways, and would eventually have a major impact on the Vietnam War. In Tonkin and Annam, the French opted for relatively indirect rule by governing through a Nguyen administrative apparatus that served as an intermediary between the French and the local population. Over time, French control over this administration became more centralized and more pervasive, but Annam and Tonkin would always remain somewhat peripheral in the French system. Poor in natural resources, the two protectorates attracted relatively little direct French economic penetration.

In Cochin China, by contrast, the French set up their own governmental structure and ruled directly – the Vietnamese who served in this system had to adhere closely to French laws and practices. The colony also experienced intensive efforts at French economic exploitation and cultural transformation. Blessed with much more arable land than Annam and Tonkin, Cochin China became the destination of choice for the French nationals who emigrated to Vietnam. Many settled in the rich Mekong Delta, and in short order the marshlands of the delta were drained and the virgin lands opened up to cultivation. Saigon, the colony's capital and commercial center, became known as the 'Paris of the Orient.' Along the border with Cambodia, rubber plantations were established. Before long, Cochin China had established itself as the most profitable, and therefore most important, part of the French empire in Southeast Asia [52; 127].

One result of this development was the emergence of an affluent Vietnamese bourgeoisie centered in Saigon, its wealth based on commerce and absentee landlordism. Many in this class were educated by the French in schools built by the French. Frequently they grew to admire French culture, eating the same food and wearing the same clothes as the *colons*. Though not averse to agitating for increased political influence and economic benefits, they generally did so within the confines of the French colonial system. But they were often scorned by these same *colons*, and many resented the European stronghold on the colony's economy. The result, as William J. Duiker has noted, was a mixture of Francophile and xenophobic instincts that gave rise to a deep ambivalence about the alleged benefits of French rule [51].

This situation deeply affected the development of the Vietnamese nationalist movement, which emerged among educated Vietnamese in the first quarter of the twentieth century. The more Francophile groups advocated non-violent reformism and were centered in Cochin China. The Constitutionalist Party, for example, founded by a small group of French-educated professionals in Saigon, voiced the Vietnamese elite's interest in changing French colonial policy without alienating the French. Vietnam, under its platform, would remain firmly within the French Union. In the 1920s the Constitutionalist Party pressed France for modest economic and political reforms, but got a chilly response. By the early 1930s, the Party was fading fast.

This failure of moderate efforts at reform gave impetus to more revolutionary approaches, especially in Annam and Tonkin. In the cities of Hanoi and Hué, and in provincial and district capitals scattered throughout Vietnam, anti-colonial elements began to form clandestine political organizations dedicated to the eviction of the French and the restoration of national independence. The Vietnamese Nationalist Party – or VNQDD, the Viet Nam Quoc Dan Dang – was the most important of these groups, and by 1929 it had some 1,500 members, most of them organized into small groups in the Red River Delta. Formed on the model of Sun Yat-sen's Nationalist Party in China, the VNQDD saw armed revolution as the lone means of gaining freedom for Vietnam, and in 1930 tried to foment a general uprising by Vietnamese serving in the French army. The effort failed, effectively ending the VNQDD's run as a nationalist group.

## HO CHI MINH

It was in this environment that the Indochinese Communist Party (ICP) emerged. Marxism had begun to win converts among some Vietnamese nationalists studying in Paris during and after World War I. Their attraction to the doctrine often had less to do with its social millenarianism than with its anti-imperialist message, promising liberation from European rule for all colonial peoples. Such was certainly the case for the founder of the party, Ho Chi Minh. Born Nguyen Sinh Cung in 1890, Ho detested French imperialism from an early age, and he vowed early to devote his life to the great task of reclaiming Vietnam for the Vietnamese people. In his early twenties he left Vietnam, marking the start of an exile that would last almost thirty years.

The journey began humbly, with Ho working on board a transport liner. After spending several years working on ships and visiting several countries, including Britain and the United States (he would later write about the brutal racial discrimination against blacks in the American South), he went to Paris near the conclusion of World War I. He immersed himself in the political activities of anti-colonial nationalists living in Paris and soon became one of their leaders. In 1920, taking the pseudonym Nguyen Ai Quoc (Nguyen the Patriot), Ho became a founding member of the French Communist Party after reading Lenin's 'Theses on the National and Colonial Questions,' a document which, in his own words, attracted him as a means of liberating Vietnam and other oppressed countries from colonial rule. Earlier, Ho had been ignored when he asked Allied leaders gathered at Versailles to grant self-determination to colonial peoples in accordance with US President Woodrow Wilson's famous Fourteen Points.

Years later, Ho reminisced about his introduction to Lenin: 'What emotion, enthusiasm, clear-sightedness and confidence it instilled in me! I was overjoyed. Though sitting alone in my room I shouted aloud as if addressing large crowds: "Dear martyrs, compatriots! This is what we need, this is our path to liberation" ' [*139 p. 14*].

In late 1923, after repeatedly failing to get the French Communist Party to take action on the colonial question, Ho Chi Minh moved to Moscow. The Soviet leadership was, however, preoccupied with domestic struggles; some officials, notably Stalin, also questioned Ho's Marxist commitment. It took Ho almost a year to convince Soviet officials to send him to southern China – where he hoped to begin organizing the Vietnamese to rise up against the French colonialists – and when he ultimately went it was without Stalin's imprimatur. In Canton Ho officially served as an interpreter for the Comintern's advisory mission to Sun Yat-sen's government. But he had a more important task: to organize the first Marxist revolutionary organization in Indochina. For the remainder of the decade, Ho worked hard to band radical intellectuals throughout Vietnam into a transitional organization called the Revolutionary Youth League of Vietnam. He also edited a political journal, *Thanh Nien* (Youth), and wrote a book titled *The Road to Revolution*, which became a bible of the revolutionary movement. Then, early in 1930, Ho Chi Minh presided over the creation of a Viet-namese communist Party in Hong Kong. Eight months later, in October, on Moscow's instructions, it was renamed the Indochinese Communist Party (ICP), with responsibility for facilitating revolutionary activity throughout French Indochina [99; 115].

From the start, the ICP was a leading force in the Vietnamese nation-alist movement. French security services immediately singled it out as the most serious threat to colonial authority, devoting most of their resources to identifying the Party's membership. What was the secret behind this domination by the ICP in the movement? In part it had to do with the weaknesses of its rivals, the non-communist nationalist groups. Despite the intensity of the Vietnamese national identity, an intensity arguably stronger than in any other society in Southeast Asia, the other anti-colonialist parties in Vietnam were plagued almost from the beginning with deep factional splits and the absence of a mass base.

To be sure, internal divisions were a common feature in many anti-colonial movements throughout the Third World and had many causes, including personality clashes and disputes over strategy. In some places, such as India and Malaya, the differences were overcome and leaders were able to form a broad alliance against the colonial power. Not so in Vietnam. Here the regional and tactical differences just proved too deep, or the personality clashes too severe, for nationalist parties to achieve unity. Moreover, anti-communist political parties in Vietnam never could establish close ties with the mass of the population. With their urban roots and middle-class concerns, party leaders tended to adopt a blasé attitude toward the issues vital to Vietnamese peasants, such as land hunger, high taxes, and government corruption.

All this left the door open to Ho Chi Minh and the ICP. Ho and his top lieutenants survived all French efforts to eliminate them, and in the mid-1930s the Party benefited from changes in the international scene. From 1936 to 1939 pressure from French authorities eased as a Popular Front government in Paris allowed communist parties in the colonies an increased measure of freedom – the result of an increased cooperation between the Soviet Union and the Western democracies against the common threat of global fascism. In 1939, however, after Moscow signed a non-aggression pact with Nazi Germany, French authorities outlawed the ICP and forced its leaders into hiding.

Many of them went to Cao Bang province on the Chinese border. There, in a cave near the village of Pac Bo in May and June 1941, the Eighth Plenum of the ICP gathered to discuss the situation in Vietnam and to plot strategy. France had surrendered to Germany in June 1940; Japan, allied with Germany, was assuming full control of the colony. The delegates sat on simple wood blocks around a bamboo table, and out of their discussions a new party came into being. Its official title was Viet Nam Doc Lap Dong Minh Hoi, or the Revolutionary League for the Independence of Vietnam – or, for history, the Vietminh. Most of the delegates were dedicated communists, but they were also ardent nationalists, and led by Ho Chi Minh they set the basic policy that would enable this small minority to capture the seething nationalism of Vietnam and make it theirs. The result would ultimately spell disaster for two of the world's leading powers, first France and then the United States.

Ho wanted the Vietminh to seek the dual objectives of national independence for Vietnam and the implementation of major social reform. But he gave primacy to the former goal. National liberation was the most important problem facing the Vietnamese people, he believed, and he felt strongly that the Vietminh had to be a patriotic, broad-based movement. The emphasis on patriotism can be seen in the organization's name, which not only stressed the issue of independence but replaced the word *Indochina* with the more emotionally charged *Vietnam*.

This was important. Ho Chi Minh was a communist, but he was first and foremost a nationalist. Liberation for his country was the one idea that never left his mind in all the years of travel, of exile, of prison. That most potent force in Vietnam, the longing to be free from foreign domination, to be independent again, would become the property of the Vietminh. The emphasis on national liberation would appeal to patriotic intellectuals, and was directed against both French colonial rule and the growing Japanese presence in the country. In June 1941, a widely circulated letter authored by Ho emphasized the nationalist foundation of the movement he led [*Doc. 1*].

And so the Vietminh was launched. Ho Chi Minh's timing was fortuitous, for the launching of the revolution coincided with the uniquely favorable circumstances of World War II. The Japanese had allowed French officials to retain nominal power in Vietnam throughout most of the war, but the swiftness with which Japan conquered the country discredited the French in the eyes of many Vietnamese. The repressive policies of the Japanese and their French puppets, along with a devastating famine early in 1945, fanned popular discontent. In northern Vietnam, Vietminh strength grew, with Ho and his close associate Vo Nguyen Giap, a former professor of history, raising an army of 5,000 men [126].

The army was swiftly put to use. On 9 March 1945, the Japanese abruptly seized control of the Indochina government, thereby ending five years of collaboration with French authorities. The Vietminh, with limited aid from a US intelligence unit, in short order began systematically to harass the new colonial master. When Japan capitulated after the atomic bombings of Hiroshima and Nagasaki in August, the Vietminh acted immediately to fill the vacuum, occupying government headquarters in Hanoi. Events moved very fast. Vietnam underwent a nationalist revolution, the so-called August Revolution, as throughout the country Vietminh associations took control of local, district, and provincial governments. In Saigon a provincial council, comprising religious sectarians, various communist splinter groups, and several non-communist nationalist groups, declared its support for the Vietminh. Between 18 and 28 August, Vietminh supporters took control of some sixty district and provincial capitals, and on the 29th the Vietminh formed a national government they called the Provisional Government of the Democratic Republic of Vietnam (DRV), with its capital in Hanoi.

It was a glorious fortnight for the Vietminh leadership, and on 2 September Ho Chi Minh, wearing the faded khaki suit and rubber sandals that had become his trademark, stood before cheering throngs in Hanoi's Ba Dinh Square and proclaimed the independence of his country. He declared: 'We hold truths that all men are created equal, that they are endowed by their Creator with certain unalienable rights, among these are Life, Liberty, and the Pursuit of Happiness' [*Doc. 2*].

Was this a sincere homage to the first of the modern statements of national independence and individual rights, or was it a play for American support for Ho's ambitions? No doubt some of both. And Ho could be forgiven for believing that the US–Vietminh collaboration in fighting the

Japanese might continue in peacetime. During the celebration that day, a band of US aircraft overflew Ba Dinh Square, and US Army officers stood with Giap and other Vietminh leaders on the reviewing stand as Vietminh forces paraded by. A Vietnamese band played *The Star Spangled Banner*. By October, a Vietnam–America Friendship Association was established with much fanfare in Hanoi. Moreover, Ho Chi Minh knew that in earlier years US President Franklin Roosevelt (FDR) had expressed support for Indochina's independence from what he considered France's exploitative and irresponsible rule. Roosevelt's view derived from his low opinion of France's performance in the struggle against the Axis, as well as his dislike of de Gaulle, who was leader of the Free French during the war and first president of the Fourth Republic. FDR considered de Gaulle 'snooty' and arrogant and looked askance at what he considered the Frenchman's obsession with restoring French grandeur after the war. All in all, then, Vietminh leaders had some reason to expect support from the United States as they sought to consolidate their power.

Behind the scenes, however, there were problems. Even as American officers joined in the celebrations in Hanoi on 2 September, their superiors back in Washington were clearing the way for a return of the French to Vietnam. Roosevelt had died in April of that year, and in his final months his position on French colonialism had shifted, partly because of his paternalistic belief that the Vietnamese were unprepared for self-rule and would therefore need a period of foreign tutelage, and partly because of growing concerns in Washington, particularly among Europeanists in the State Department, that gaining French and British cooperation in Europe would require a less hostile attitude toward their colonial empires. Roosevelt quietly shelved the nettlesome Indochina issue in the final months of his life, clearing the way for a French return after the war. The new president, Harry S. Truman, regarded with distaste the French effort to regain control. But he did not share his predecessor's concern about colonialism in general, or his interest in Southeast Asia in particular [54; 93; 202].

As a result, when French leaders moved to reassert control of Indochina in the autumn of 1945 – their compulsion derived from a belief that their future as a great power was at stake – American officials did not stand in their way. Under an Allied plan, British troops entered the southern part of Vietnam to disarm the defeated Japanese, while Chinese Nationalist forces arrived in the north to perform the same function. The British, concerned about losing their own colonies and not wanting Vietnam to set any precedents, released and rearmed interned French soldiers, who promptly clashed with Vietminh forces. New French units landed to reassert France's authority in the south.

Ho Chi Minh recognized his government's isolation. The Americans, who had embraced the August Revolution, had departed, and his several appeals to the United States for support had gone unanswered [*Doc. 3*]. Great Britain would be no help, he knew. The Chinese Nationalists, about to leave the scene as well, had agreed to let French forces enter the north, and the French already had an invasion force off the coast near Haiphong. Even the Soviet Union, the leading communist power, seemed to take no interest in the Vietminh's cause. As Ho learned of the Paris government's plans to send troops to northern Vietnam, he knew that the Vietminh faced the prospect of fighting a war against a much better equipped French army, and with virtually no outside support.

Desperate to avert war, Ho in the spring of 1946 offered concessions to the French. He agreed to permit them to return to the north to displace the Chinese. He also agreed to affiliate an autonomous Vietnam with the French Union, a loose federation of states linked to France. In return, French negotiator Jean Sainteny pledged that there would be a national referendum to determine whether Cochin China would rejoin Annam and Tonkin in a reunited Vietnam or remain a separate French territory. The two sides also agreed that a Vietminh delegation would travel to Paris later in the year to settle outstanding questions regarding the nature of Vietnamese independence and the timing of the election regarding Cochin China [*Doc. 4*] [73; 178].

And so, in the summer of 1946, French and Vietnamese delegates met for a series of talks at Fontainebleau near Paris. The outcome would be disastrous. To most Frenchmen war was unthinkable, but the alternative, giving away independence to 'little yellow men' (*les jaunes*) who could be so easily dominated, was even more unimaginable. The Paris government was unyielding in the talks. The old problems remained unchanged: the Vietnamese wanted independence and a weak form of association with France; Paris sought guided self-government for Vietnam within the French Union, with France controlling the sovereignty of Vietnam – in other words, the French would control the crucial ministries. Days and weeks passed, and the gap between Ho Chi Minh and his hosts never seemed to narrow. David Ben Gurion, the great Israeli leader, described it this way:

> The French had given Ho a giant red carpet when he first arrived (customary for a visiting chief of state). But Ho's descending fortunes in the negotiations could be measured by the progressive shrinking of the carpet. On Ho's arrival it had extended from the sidewalk to his room. As the summer wore on, it was limited to the lobby, then to the staircase, and finally simply to the corridor in front of Ho's suite. [82 *p. 89*]

An American journalist, David Schoenbrun, asked Ho what he would do if the French did not give him some form of independence.

'President Ho, what will you do?'
'Why, we will fight of course,' Ho replied.

'But President Ho,' Schoenbrun continued, 'the French are a powerful nation. They have airplanes and tanks and modern weapons. You have no modern weapons, no tanks, no airplanes. Not even uniforms. How can you fight them?'

'We will be like the elephant and the tiger,' Ho responded. 'When the elephant is strong and rested and near his base we will retreat. And if the tiger ever pauses, the elephant will impale him with his mighty tusks. But the tiger will not and the elephant will die of exhaustion and the loss of blood.' [Cited in 82 *p. 89*]

In September 1946 the two sides finally signed an agreement, but it was basically an agreement to disagree, a decision that solved nothing. His red carpet gone, Ho left Paris, sure that war was coming. The French had not granted independence; now, he realized, he would have to fight for it.


THE FRANCO-VIETMINH WAR

War broke out in Vietnam in November 1946. The occasion was a French claim to jurisdiction in enforcing customs regulations against Chinese smugglers whom the Vietnamese were willing to accommodate. Following two days of fighting between French and Vietminh forces at Haiphong, the port of Hanoi, Ho Chi Minh and his associates took to the hills, announcing that they would fight for the independence of Vietnam and its reunification until both objectives were achieved. The French themselves filled any positions vacated by Vietnamese officials and set up a special administration for the backward and impoverished Moi population in the hill country of southern Annam bordering on Cochin China, thus virtually detaching this area from the rest of the country [178]. On 19 December, General Vo Nguyen Giap, commander of Vietminh forces, ordered a war of national resistance.

Giap's forces had the triple advantage of fighting experience won during the last phases of the Japanese occupation, of occasional material aid from Mao Zedong's Communists in China, and of operating in a region where the population was on their side. It soon became clear that the French would have difficulty in defeating them by conventional military means. Short of a series of genuine transfers of executive and legislative authority to the Vietnamese government, there could be little hope of early pacification, and Paris was still not prepared to yield more than a titular independence without the substance of even a true autonomy. A modicum of self-government was to be available only for administrations willing to cooperate with the French on French terms.

Yet the French understood that it would be important to try to find such an administration. Accordingly, in June 1948 there emerged the first central government for Vietnam in opposition to the government of Ho Chi

Minh. Largely a French creation, it had no following whatsoever in the country but the French negotiated with it their first (abortive) agreement promising independence and unity for Vietnam. Then in March 1949 another agreement was struck, this time with Bao Dai, a former emperor who had recently returned to public life. The Elysée Agreement granted 'independence' to the 'State of Vietnam,' Laos, and Cambodia, which became 'associated states' within the French Union. The deal allowed Paris to portray the war as a conflict between a free Vietnam and the communists – and therefore not a colonial war at all.

Thus there were now two rival governments in Vietnam, one bent on achieving independence before regulating its relations with France by treaty, the other counting on the attainment of independence by gradual means through close association with France. The Ho Chi Minh government, which enjoyed wide popular support in the south as well as in the north, regarded the Vietnam which had entered the French Union as a wholly illegitimate entity, but it was unable itself to establish administrative control in any of the territory held by French military forces. The Bao Dai government, on the other hand, desperately in need of public support, argued that the true Vietnam was the country whose reunification Bao Dai had secured by negotiation. Genuine nationalists should rally to his banner since he, rather than Ho, was in the best position to win independence for the Vietnamese. This he would do by patient diplomacy and non-violent political progress, not by destructive warfare. Unfortunately for Bao Dai, however, his government continued to have relatively little popularity, and depended on French support in the south as well as in the north for its day-to-day survival.

The French proved to be mistaken in believing that limited concessions to nationalist sentiment made in the March 1949 agreement with Bao Dai would draw off popular support from Ho Chi Minh and thus enable them to defeat him. On the contrary the conflict in Indochina now entered a new and much more dangerous phase. As a result of their victory over Chiang Kai-Shek, the Chinese Communists were free after the closing weeks of 1949 to extend more aid than before to the DRV. The Chinese supplied arms and equipment to the Vietminh, and also provided Chinese sanctuaries in which the Vietminh could train and replenish their troops. Plenty of arms were available from the large stock of weapons the United States had sent to Chiang Kai-Shek's Nationalist forces [85].

Ho Chi Minh had less success winning support from the other great powers. Neither the United States nor Great Britain accepted his appeals for assistance. More and more, Washington officials saw Indochina not as a colonial issue but as part of the global anti-communist struggle. The principal threat to American security and world peace, they believed, was monolithic, dictatorial communism emanating from the Soviet Union. Any communist anywhere, whether home or abroad, was a witting or unwitting agent of Moscow. Little wonder, then, that the Truman administration should ignore no fewer than eight requests for aid from Ho Chi Minh. Ho and his chief lieutenants were communists with long-standing ties to the Soviet Union. They were also ardent nationalists who had fought first to rid Vietnam of the Japanese and then, after Tokyo's surrender in mid-1945, to prevent France from re-establishing its mastery over the country, but this mattered much less to the powers that be in Washington. As the US secretary of state Dean Acheson put it in May 1949, 'the question [of] whether Ho [is] as much nationalist as Commie is irrelevant. All Stalinists in colonial areas are nationalists.'

The American conception of Vietnam as a Cold War battleground largely ignored the struggle for social justice and national sovereignty occurring within the country. Moreover, the fixation with Ho Chi Minh's communist background existed despite the fact that the USSR took virtually no interest in the Indochina struggle or the Vietminh's problems. Moscow did not extend diplomatic recognition to the Democratic Republic of Vietnam that Ho proclaimed in August 1945, and instead continued to regard France as the legitimate ruler of Indochina. Much as Washington viewed the Vietnamese revolution through the prism of European developments, so did Stalin; he granted little importance to the aspirations of obscure comrades in a small country that had never been of geostrategic or economic importance to the Soviet Union. It is also possible that his long-standing suspicions of Ho's ideological purity, which dated back to the 1920s, influenced his aloofness toward the revolution. Finally there was the matter of the French Communist Party, whose power Stalin hoped to see grow. The Party in the early years supported the government's get-tough policy in Indochina, which no doubt further inclined Stalin to acquiesce in France's suppression of the Vietnamese communists.

In the early years of the Franco-Vietminh War, therefore, France could count on the non-interference of both of the world's superpowers and, in the case of the Americans, tacit support. The Vietminh were isolated warriors. Not until the communist take-over in China would they have significant outside support. In addition, they had no navy or air force, and only a third of their 150,000 soldiers were equipped with even small arms; on the other side, France came with a well-armed and well-trained force of 100,000.

Logic dictated it would be a rout. But the war nevertheless went badly for the French. Although they retained control of most cities and major towns, and with their superior firepower were able to defeat the Vietminh in open battles, they proved unable to achieve a military victory. In the countryside, where the vast majority of the population lived, the Vietminh reigned supreme, assured as they were of the staunch support of the peasantry. One French official thought it would take a French force of at least 500,000 to overcome this Vietminh stranglehold on the rural areas, and advised against the attempt. Another said the keys to victory were political, not military. 'Anti-communism will be a useless tool as long as the problem of nationalism remains unsolved,' he said, which meant that the 'capital problem from now is political. It is a question of coming to terms with an awakening xenophobic nationalism' [44; 60].

There were large lessons here for the American backers of the French war effort, but few in Washington thought to consider them. Many were inclined to blame France's military performance and colonialist motivation for its troubles in the war. Most thought there was still time to turn things around. Virtually all deemed it necessary to try. In early 1950, after the communist victory in China but prior to the outbreak of the Korean War, the Truman administration made the first step toward direct US involvement in Indochina – it opted to prop up an embattled colonial regime in order to prevent a communist victory and also to retain French support in the European theater of the Cold War. In February the administration granted diplomatic recognition to a puppet government headed by the former emperor, Bao Dai. In early March it pledged to furnish France with military and economic assistance for the war effort. The outbreak of the Korean War in late spring, together with concern about the intentions of the Chinese communists, solidified Washington's commitment [*Doc. 5*] [69].

The American aid decision came at a pivotal time. The drain on French resources caused by the war was exceedingly heavy, affecting both the rate of national recovery from World War II and the ability of France to contribute to European reorganization and to the work of the North Atlantic Treaty Organization (NATO). US assistance to the war effort would henceforth be vital, French officials knew. Moreover, the communist victory in China changed the nature of the Franco-Vietminh War, adding to the pressure on France. Emboldened by China's material and rhetorical support, Vietminh General Vo Nguyen Giap staged daring offensives, but he was stopped by French forces under General Jean de Lattre de Tassigny, who inspired his troops to fight vigorously. But de Lattre, sick with stomach cancer, retired and soon died, and his successors lacked his ability.

## DIEN BIEN PHU

As time passed and the prospects for the French war effort grew worse rather than better, proposals for withdrawal from Indochina began to be heard more and more frequently in France, even outside leftist circles. These proposals were rejected by the government. Withdrawal of French Union forces, it insisted, would be followed by a general massacre of thousands of French civilians and the extermination of the Vietnamese elements co-operating with the Bao Dai administration. It would also have a disastrous effect on the morale of elements resisting the advance of communism elsewhere in Southeast Asia. The government still maintained that its policy of holding on in Indochina was a practical one, arguing that the war-weary Vietnamese were bound sooner or later to accept any arrangement which promised a stable regime and security and that sooner or later they might be expected to rally to Bao Dai if the communists could only be held back by military action a little longer.

So the war continued, while the United States kept on raising the level of its material aid until American taxpayers were carrying by the spring of 1954 about three-quarters of the financial cost of the French effort. Bombers, cargo planes, trucks, tanks, naval craft, automatic weapons, small arms and ammunition, radios, hospital and engineering equipment plus financial aid flowed heavily. Between 1950 and 1954 US investment in the war in Indochina reached a total of approximately $3 billion.

On the diplomatic front, Washington applied intense pressure on the newly independent countries in South and Southeast Asia to recognize the Bao Dai government. Major efforts were made in India, Burma, the Philippines, and Thailand to affect regional perceptions of Bao Dai, but most of these states remained non-commital. Their leaders tended to see the conflict in Vietnam as a nationalist struggle against colonialism, finding it much less easy than the Truman administration to overlook France's unwillingness to grant Vietnam full independence. Even the leadership of the former US colony of the Philippines dragged its feet, which prompted Secretary of State Dean Acheson to say 'This general indifference or lack of understanding may prove to be disastrous for those nations as Communism relentlessly advances. It is impossible to help them resist Communism if they are not prepared to help themselves' [20 *p. 181*]. It was a lament that would be repeated time and again by Acheson's successors in the years that followed.

The Vietminh, meanwhile, received important assistance from the Soviet Union and China, though its relations with both communist powers were often fractious. In 1950, when Ho Chi Minh traveled with Mao Zedong and Zhou Enlai by train to Moscow in the hope of gaining Soviet support for the war against the French, Stalin treated him with contempt. At the ceremony to sign a Sino-Soviet pact, Ho suggested that Stalin sign a similar agreement with Vietnam. The Soviet leader replied that because Ho was in Moscow on an unofficial visit, this wasn't possible. Ho proposed, perhaps in jest, that he be flown around Moscow in a helicopter and then land with suitable pomp, whereupon Stalin snapped, 'Oh, you Orientals. You have such rich imaginations' [51].

Stalin subsequently did recognize the DRV that year, and he agreed to deliver material assistance to the Vietminh in the war against the French on the condition that China play a prominent role in directing the struggle. Ho

Chi Minh was wary. He and Vo Nguyen Giap certainly welcomed Beijing's material assistance in the war against France, but Ho had little desire to see a heavy Chinese influence on the Vietminh's internal ideological debates. He became unhappy with the hard-line revolutionary stance pushed by Mao's advisers and grew more and more wary of falling under the kind of Chinese tutelage he had always resisted in the past. For the remainder of the Franco-Vietminh War he would work hard to keep the Chinese at arm's length.

In mid-1953 the French won American support for an ambitious military plan advanced by General Henri Navarre, who had recently been named commander of French forces in Indochina. The Navarre Plan called for sending an additional ten French battalions to Indochina and boosting significantly the native segment of the armed forces; this new larger army would then mount a major offensive to drive the Vietminh from their stronghold in the Red River Delta. But Navarre committed a grave strategic error. Determined to prevent Ho's forces from invading neighboring Laos, Navarre in late 1953 chose to block them at Dien Bien Phu, a remote outpost near the Laotian border. Contrary to French expectations, Vo Nguyen Giap equipped his men with artillery provided by China, and they were able to trap the French garrison in the valley [59; 85].

With public opinion in France wavering under the strain of high casualty lists and military setbacks, Paris tried in early 1954 to secure direct American air intervention to relieve the beleaguered French garrison. Washington leaders, aware that a French defeat at Dien Bien Phu might lead to France's withdrawal from Indochina, faced the uncomfortable fact that only US intervention might save the day. Indochina's strategic importance remained a given: virtually no one questioned that communist domination of Vietnam would weaken non-communist governments throughout Southeast Asia, with far-reaching ramifications. At a press conference on 5 April President Dwight D. Eisenhower gave public expression to these concerns in what was to become one of the most frequently cited justifications for US involvement in Vietnam in the decade that followed – the so-called 'domino theory,' in which the fall of one country in the region to communism would cause others to tumble swiftly as well. Knock over one domino and the rest would soon follow [*Doc. 6*].

Yet despite Indochina's perceived strategic importance, the Eisenhower administration decided against intervention on behalf of the French. Dwight Eisenhower privately called the French 'a hopeless, helpless mass of protoplasm,' but he was no less inclined than Truman had been to see the French struggle as an extension of America's Cold War effort [1]. He and his secretary of state, John Foster Dulles, gave serious consideration to the French request, asking Congress in April for authority to use, if necessary, US troops to save the French position. The lawmakers, including Democratic senator Lyndon Baines Johnson from Texas, refused to go along unless the British also joined. (In a remark that would take on a haunting tone a decade later, they warned that there must be 'no more Koreas with the United States furnishing 90 per cent of the manpower.') They also insisted that France had to pledge to move swiftly to grant Vietnam independence. This Congressional attitude effectively left the matter in the hands of the British, who declined to participate on the grounds that the intervention might precipitate a disastrous war with Communist China if not with the Soviet Union too. London officials did not believe in any case that an air strike would be enough to salvage the situation, and they were not inclined to put much stock in the notion of falling dominoes [15; 23].

On 7 May 1954, the French capitulated at Dien Bien Phu. The next day, an international conference already in session in Geneva began to discuss a basis for a cease-fire in the war. Although the conflict was approaching its climax and Vietminh leaders vowed to continue fighting until they won a definitive victory, there was reason to hope that a negotiated settlement might be possible. A *détente* in relations between East and West suited the general policy of the Soviet Union at the time. Neutralist Asian states greatly desired an end to the conflict in Indochina, which was retarding the national development of newly emancipated countries in South and Southeast Asia. China was anxious to establish diplomatic relations with uncommitted Asian states from which it was still isolated and the war was retarding the desired *rapprochement*. Nor did the Chinese want to continue indefinitely matching in Indochina the stepped-up pace of US military aid, with the attendant risk of a general war. They apparently believed, moreover, that the Vietminh hold on Indochina was already strong enough to ensure that communist interests would be well served there in the future. France itself was losing the will to continue a war which it obviously could not win. Several NATO powers thought Paris should cut its losses in Southeast Asia and concentrate its attention instead on the reorganization of Europe.

The Eisenhower administration, however, felt differently. The senior American representative at Geneva, Secretary of State John Foster Dulles, had grave misgivings about the negotiations, and he encouraged the French to continue the struggle in Indochina in the interest of the 'free world.' The French, under new prime minister Pierre Mendès France, refused, and in July a peace settlement would be signed. But the position adopted by the United States during the talks would influence greatly the specifics of the accords, and help set the stage for renewed conflict. The Geneva Accords had brought to an end the Franco-Vietminh War, but another Western power readied to enter the scene.

# CHAPTER THREE

# THE DIEM EXPERIMENT

## THE GENEVA CONFERENCE

Dien Bien Phu was a humiliating defeat for France, coming on the heels of seven-plus years of bloody fighting and constant promises by French generals that victory was just around the corner. Remarkably, however, officials in Paris were able to accept this result with a good deal more equanimity than their counterparts across the Atlantic. When Paris policy-makers began speaking in mid-1953 of the need for an early negotiated settlement, US officials were appalled. Right up until the start of the Geneva Conference, the administration sought to stiffen the spine of the French, as when Dulles in July 1953 told the French foreign minister Georges Bidault, that no negotiations should be undertaken until the tide of battle had been turned – in other words, until France could dictate terms [54].

This notion that negotiations should never be entered into unless they could be entered into from strength had a long history in American diplomacy, but it became more pronounced after World War II, when the United States possessed unprecedented power in world affairs (top dogs seldom are much interested in compromise) and when Containment became the guiding principle of American foreign policy. Containment can be said to have marked the triumph of strategy over diplomacy, as the procurement of bases and deployment of weapons systems took precedence over bargaining, negotiation, accommodation. Communists were the children of darkness, the source of evil in the world; negotiating with them was out of the question. Containment, Henry Kissinger has written, 'allowed no role for diplomacy until the climactic final scene in which the men in the white hats accepted the conversion of the men in the black hats' [111 *p. 471*]. Unconditional surrender was required. Hence the great misgivings with which the administration approached the Geneva meeting. John Foster Dulles only reluctantly went to the conference and he made it clear he would meet with China's foreign minister Zhou Enlai only if, as he put it, their cars collided. Sure enough, when the opportunity came for the two men to shake hands, Dulles refused.

Yet the conference did not go as poorly from Washington's perspective as many US officials had feared. There is an oft-quoted axiom of military strategy which says that one can rarely win at the bargaining table what one has proved unable to achieve on the battlefield. As with many axioms, this one is not as axiomatic as it at first appears. Even a cursory glance at the wars of the twentieth century shows that the final shape of diplomatic agreements does not always reflect the overall politico-military balance on the ground. At Geneva in 1954, the Vietminh by all accounts was in a dominant military position. It had scored a decisive victory over the French at Dien Bien Phu, and it dominated most of Vietnam politically and militarily [*Doc. 7*]. In neighboring Laos the Vietminh-supported Pathet Lao independence movement controlled as much as 50 percent of the territory. France, moreover, had made it quite clear that it could not continue the war – neither French public opinion nor the leadership in Paris had the will to go on.

The final settlement at Geneva, however, did not reflect this Vietminh superiority. The accords, signed in July 1954, provided for the temporary partition of Vietnam along the seventeenth parallel – the demarcation line, it was stressed, should not be 'interpreted as constituting a political or territorial boundary' – and a Demilitarized Zone (DMZ) 10 kilometers wide along that parallel. Vietminh forces were to be regrouped north of the DMZ and French troops south of it. General elections to reunify the country were to be held in July 1956, following a year of consultations between representatives of the two zones. In addition, there were to be no troop reinforcements, no rearming, no military bases, and no foreign military alliances on the part of the administration of either zone. An International Control Commission (ICC) comprised of Canadian, Indian, and Polish representatives would supervise the terms of the accords and investigate any complaints. Laos and Cambodia were declared independent nations, with the Pathet Lao – prohibited from attending the conference – given control only of two small and underpopulated areas of Laos [*Doc. 8*] [26; 154].

In effect, Ho Chi Minh had settled for half a country, even though his forces were dominant in virtually all of it. Why did he do so? Simply put, because the key players at Geneva left him no real alternative. American officials had grave concerns about going to Geneva, but once there played a shrewd diplomatic game. They engaged in what John Foster Dulles called 'holding action' diplomacy to prevent a settlement that would give Indochina to the Vietminh. Specifically, Washington continued to issue thinly veiled threats of military intervention should it not be satisfied with the terms of the accords, and in general kept the other delegations guessing about its ultimate plans. The other two Western powers, Britain and France, did not want an American military intervention in Indochina, and were anxious to avoid alienating Washington unduly over Vietnam – too many other important Anglo-American and Franco-American bilateral issues could suffer as a result. France also wanted to retain some influence in Indochina, which the proposed division of Vietnam into two zones would allow.

The Soviet Union, meanwhile, anxious to keep France out of the US-sponsored European Defense Community (EDC), accommodated some of France's desires on Indochina as a means of reducing the French commitment to the Western alliance. Like the London and Paris governments, Moscow also sought to avert an American intervention in Vietnam, and it saw in Indochina – an area its leaders had long considered of marginal interest – an opportunity to demonstrate its commitment to 'peaceful coexistence' through compromise with the West [66].

Most important of all, China threw its weight behind the accords. Its chief representative in Geneva, the smooth and urbane foreign minister Zhou Enlai, leaned hard on the Vietminh delegation led by Pham Van Dong to accept the terms. Beijing's motivations were complex, but a key concern was the same as for the Soviets, French, and British: to avoid giving the United States an excuse to intervene in Vietnam. Hence it would be necessary to achieve a settlement that would bring at least grudging support from Washington. In addition, the Chinese sought a period of peace in the region, so that they might focus attention on China's economic development – two decades of almost constant international or civil war had taken their toll [26; 106].

Chinese and Soviet pressure on the DRV to accept a compromise settlement thus was crucial in the signing of the accords. But Hanoi, too, saw advantages in a deal. No less averse than the other powers at Geneva to forestall a US intervention, and confident that reunification of the country could be achieved by peaceful means, Pham Van Dong agreed to accept the terms of the accords. Still, it was a frustrating time for him and his Vietminh allies. There was no getting around it: they were departing from Geneva with significantly less than they came with.

American leaders, it would seem, had every reason to be pleased with the outcome of the conference. Yet they were not. They understood that they had probably gotten about as good a result as was possible, in view of the French exhaustion and the situation on the ground in Vietnam, but they were unwilling to sign the accords. Britain, France, China, the USSR, and the DRV did so; the United States and the State of Vietnam refused. Instead, Washington issued a separate statement that agreed with the general principles and promised not to 'disturb them' by the 'threat or use of force.' Eisenhower declared that the United States 'had not itself been party to or bound by the decisions taken by the conference' [1; 100].

The Eisenhower team, it is clear, wanted to preserve American freedom of action. The president and his top aides realized that the agreements, if fulfilled, worked to the advantage of Ho Chi Minh and his government. Hanoi might have been forced to withdraw its troops from southern Vietnam, Laos, and Cambodia, and to accept a division of the country, but overall it came out of Geneva in a strong position. The State of Vietnam in the south was a weak entity, with a leader in Bao Dai who had very little popular support. The DRV, meanwhile, had international sanction and a leadership that had gained immense prestige and power in taking on and defeating the French. Should the Geneva Accords be implemented and the 1956 elections held, US officials believed, the Communists would win control of the whole country.

To forestall that eventuality, Washington moved quickly in the wake of the Geneva Conference to implement a regional defense system. On 12 August 1954, the NSC met and decided that the US support of the French war had led to a serious loss of prestige. Restoring that prestige meant preventing additional losses in Southeast Asia, members agreed. The immediate task was to succeed France as the direct supplier of financial and military assistance to South Vietnam. The document that resulted from the meeting, NSC 5429/2 (approved by Eisenhower on 20 August), put the matter plainly: 'The U.S. must protect its position and restore its prestige in the Far East by a new initiative in Southeast Asia, where the situation must be stabilized as soon as possible to prevent further losses to communism through (1) creeping expansion and subversion, or (2) overt aggression.' The document concluded with a recommendation for a Southeast Asia collective security treaty and endorsed 'covert operations on a large and effective scale in support of the foregoing policies' [11].

John Foster Dulles was already thinking along similar lines. In September 1954, under his guidance, a loose defense organization had taken shape under the name Southeast Asia Treaty Organization (SEATO). Its odd assortment of members included the United States, Britain, France, Australia, and New Zealand. Only three Asian nations chose to join: Thailand, the Philippines, and Pakistan (the latter mostly because it hoped to use SEATO against its bitter foe, India). Each nation pledged that in case of an armed attack against a Southeast Asian state or territory, it would respond 'in accordance with its constitutional processes' [*Doc. 9*]. In other words, no member was obligated to do much of anything. In practice, SEATO would prove largely irrelevant, because none of the other members shared Washington's fear of the spread of communism in the region. Largely irrelevant, but not totally: for the next dozen years, as one historian has noted, 'U.S. officials used this supposed *collective* security pact to justify the *unilateral* American commitment to Vietnam' [117 *p. 524*].

A YOGI-LIKE MYSTIC

The Eisenhower team also moved energetically within South Vietnam itself in those early months after Geneva. One of the administration's stock criticisms of the French during the war had been that Paris never lent support to popular anti-communist nationalists who might have posed a real challenge to Ho Chi Minh's leadership. Now Americans had the chance to rectify this mistake. In June, in the midst of the Geneva Conference, Emperor Bao Dai, hoping to win American support for the State of Vietnam, had appointed Ngo Dinh Diem as prime minister. Bao Dai viewed Diem as 'difficult' because of his fanaticism and messianistic tendencies, but he hoped that Washington would appreciate Diem's virulent opposition to communism. Several other observers already viewed Diem as being 'in the American pocket.' This was an exaggeration, but US officials certainly hoped that in Diem they had found the man around whom they could construct a non-communist bastion in the South.

An ascetic bachelor, Diem was born into a Catholic family in the imperial capital of Hué in 1901. He attended the prestigious National Academy and then took a law degree from the University of Hanoi. Entering the civil service upon graduation, Diem rose rapidly through the ranks, becoming minister of the interior in the government of Emperor Bao Dai in 1933. He resigned a few months later in protest against French unwillingness to grant Vietnam greater autonomy.

For the next two decades, Diem remained inactive in politics. An ardent Catholic, he resolutely opposed communism, and in late 1945 he refused an offer from Ho Chi Minh to collaborate with the Vietminh. In 1950, Diem rejected Bao Dai's offer of the prime ministership of the State of Vietnam, and he embarked on a series of travels to Japan, Europe, and the United States, where he spent two years at the Maryknoll Seminary in New Jersey. This long hiatus from public life, coupled with his ascetic and reclusive lifestyle, made Diem an unlikely candidate for national leadership. But his name continued to carry considerable influence in Vietnam, and he made contacts with numerous influential Americans while in the United States, among them Francis Cardinal Spellman, Justice William O. Douglas, and Senators Mike Mansfield and John F. Kennedy. In mid-1954, with his country about to be partitioned by the conferees in Geneva, Diem raced to Saigon. This time he accepted Bao Dai's offer.

American officials were unenthusiastic about Diem's advent to power, for they knew of his reclusive, arrogant nature and lack of popular support. One US diplomat called him a 'messiah without a message.' Another observed that Diem 'may have little to offer other than to reiterate that the solution of the Vietnamese problem depends on the increased responsibility by the U.S.' [54 *p. 196*]. A psychological profile of Diem described him as distrustful of the advice of anyone outside his own family. He spent long hours alone, meditating. He was never comfortable around women, and intelligence analysts made much of the fact that they had no evidence he had ever had sexual relations.

For all of his weaknesses, however, Diem appeared to most American officials to be better than any other possible contender for the leadership of South Vietnam, and so they threw their lot behind him. One US analyst summarized Washington's dilemma: 'We are prepared to accept the seemingly ridiculous prospect that this yogi-like mystic could assume the charge he is apparently about to undertake only because the standard set by his predecessors is so low' [94 *p. 55*].

From the start, the administration gave top priority to building a South Vietnamese army. John Foster Dulles called it an essential first step in promoting a stable government. The withdrawal of the French, the presence of a large, experienced army in the North, and continued instability in the South, all underscored the need for a strong army. Between 1955 and 1961, military assistance constituted more than 78 percent of the total American foreign aid program to South Vietnam.

FRICTIONS IN THE WEST

Signs of Washington's increasing role in the war, signified by its support for Diem, caused growing friction with the French in the last months of 1954 and into 1955. The French and American partnership in Indochina had always been riven with tension and mutual mistrust, and the friction did not end with Geneva. French premier Mendès France wanted to cooperate with Washington as much as possible, and in the wake of the Geneva Conference the two countries tried to cooperate to establish a viable government in Saigon, but long-term differences of approach plagued the effort. Both sides saw the weaknesses of Ngo Dinh Diem, but whereas Washington still sought to work with him, Paris preferred to reject him altogether in favor of someone less anti-French – and, the French were quick to add, more able to lead a government. When the French delayed turning over full powers of governance to Diem until December, US policymakers suspected that Paris was trying to retain control in the South and also build bridges to Hanoi. American officials also knew that France was aiding Diem's political rivals and trying to undermine Diem. As if that were not enough, Franco-American friction was exacerbated by the French rejection of membership in the EDC a month after Geneva.

Nor was it merely the French who disagreed with Washington on the best result for Indochina in mid-1954 and on the broader issue of negotiating with communists. The British government, likewise, entered the conference with a different conception of what should happen. London and

Washington were in general agreement on the need to check the spread of communism in Southeast Asia, but not on the means of doing so. To the British, it was imperative that the 1956 elections called for in the Geneva Accords should actually take place, even if that would result in a victory by Ho Chi Minh. In British eyes, a unified Titoist Vietnam seemed a reasonable objective, particularly given the likely alternative of continued instability and eventual war. When Washington immediately after the conference set about subverting the accords – substituting American influence for French and attempting to change the truce line into a permanent boundary – London officials were disturbed, and their frustration increased as it appeared Diem would decide to forgo the 1956 elections. Alarmist American references to 'appeasement' and 'the lessons of Munich' did not impress these officials; that analogy simply could not be stretched to the Southeast Asia of the 1950s, in their view. The same applied to frequent White House references to the notion of falling dominoes, the idea that the 'loss' of Vietnam would cause the collapse of all of Southeast Asia. The British did not think the outcome of their own adventure in Malaya depended on what happened in Vietnam [34; 56].

As early as the mid-point of the 1950s, then, we find early signs of what a decade later would become such a pronounced feature of international opinion about Vietnam: the isolation of the United States from key members of the Western world. As in the later case, the differences were not always visible – in both time-periods Britain chose to avoid confronting Washington over the issue – but they were real. As then, even many Asian nations were dubious about American aims. Recall that SEATO, announced with such fanfare in the fall of 1954, contained only two Southeast Asian members, Thailand and the Philippines. India and Indonesia, the most important South and Southeast Asian states, rejected membership, as did Burma.

Geneva and its aftermath also revealed the undoubted importance of domestic political considerations in the making of American policy. Here, too, the connection to the 1963–65 period is considerable. There can be no doubt that one reason the administration worked so hard to distance itself from the Geneva agreement was that it feared it might get a hostile reaction from outspoken anti-communists in Congress. Only four years had passed since the attack on Truman for 'losing' China, and the prospect of a repeat of that ordeal must have hung heavy over the Eisenhower team. The shadow of Joseph McCarthy still loomed large.

As it happened, the domestic backlash to the accords was relatively slight. Republican senator William Knowland of California denounced the settlement as the 'greatest victory the Communists have won in twenty years,' and Cardinal Spellman spoke of the 'newly betrayed millions of Indochinese' who now had 'to learn the awful facts of slavery from their eager Communist masters.' Overall, however, the response to the agreement was muted, which suggests either that the White House strategy paid off or, intriguingly, that the Vietnam issue did not yet animate the minds of most opinion-makers, or some combination of the two [54; 91].

At the very least, domestic political concerns made administration officials resort to apocalyptic rhetoric in justifying their policies, which in turn made them appear more naive than they really were.

## AMERICAN REALISM?

This brings us to yet another similarity between 1954–55 and 1964–65: the considerable amount of realism that existed at the top levels of American decision-making. Senior officials knew they faced major obstacles in nation-building in South Vietnam. They knew the Vietminh represented a formidable foe. They had more faith in the capacities of Ngo Dinh Diem than did the French and British, but not all that much more; the Eisenhower team, as we have seen, had concerns about him from the start, concerns about his lack of political realism, his intellectual rigidity, his Catholic religion in a nation overwhelmingly Buddhist. The Central Intelligence Agency (CIA), whose analysis of the political and military situation stands up as remarkably accurate throughout this whole period, regularly warned of major obstacles ahead; if not all of this analysis found its way to the inner sanctum of power, some of it certainly did.

In a candid moment John Foster Dulles put the chances of success for the South Vietnam gamble at about 10 percent – hardly a sign of optimism. William J. Duiker, a careful student of this period, puts it well when he asserts that the Eisenhower administration 'went into the Diem experiment with its eyes wide open' [54 *p. 211*]. As would be the case a decade later, where policy-makers differed from the skeptics was not so much in their diagnosis, or even their prognosis, but in their prescription. As then, it was at the prescription stage that they proved, in both periods, inflexible, unimaginative, myopic.

This connection between American official thinking about Vietnam in the early and mid-1950s and the mid-1960s, and the important constants that remained throughout, should not be drawn too closely. The Truman and Eisenhower records in Vietnam were not good ones, and they bear a good deal of responsibility for the war that in the 1960s and 1970s would claim so many hundreds of thousands of lives and cause so much destruction to large parts of Indochina. Their policy decisions laid the critical foundation for what happened later. But the misjudgments and policy failures of this earlier period, though considerable and though perceived as such by some at the time, were more understandable, more reasonable than those that were made in the critical months of 1963 and 1964 and 1965.

Many of the fundamental assumptions – about Vietnam's importance, about the obstacles ahead, about the cost of withdrawal – may have been similar, but they made sense in the first half of the 1950s in a way they would not a decade later. In retrospect, the Truman administration was on the wrong side of history when it sided with the French against the Vietminh, but the 1950 aid decision makes a good deal of sense when one considers that it came in the wake of the 'twin shocks' of 1949 – the Soviet detonation of an atomic bomb and the communist victory in China – and at a time when French cooperation in Europe still seemed vital.

Likewise, though American strategists in the period after Geneva were mistaken to reject out of hand the notion of a unified Titoist Vietnam, their reasoning for doing so was not altogether spurious. The perceived success of anti-communist operations in Greece in 1947, Iran in 1953, Guatemala in 1954, and the Philippines in the same year quite naturally led some American officials to believe that they could pull it off again, that they could in that way have something better than Titoism; in the mid-1960s this was a much more dubious proposition. Eisenhower and Dulles were too dismissive of the lessons that the French defeat held for any Western power that came after, but this is far more understandable in their case than in the case of the Kennedy and Johnson crowds.

Even the decision to throw full support behind Diem, which encountered objections not merely from London and Paris but also some high-ranking Americans (notably General J. Lawton Collins, the special US representative to Vietnam with the rank of ambassador), could be defended in the context of what was known at the time. Eisenhower and Dulles could and did argue that, whatever his weaknesses, Diem's stubborn anti-colonialism and single-mindedness might prove to be just the qualities South Vietnam needed in a leader. Moreover, neither the French nor the British nor anyone else could come up with an alternative to Diem, which lessened the power of their critique considerably. All in all, then, making a stand in the southern part of Vietnam was not an illogical move in 1954, given the globalization of the Cold War, given the domestic political realities, and, most of all perhaps, given that the costs seemed reasonable – a few hundred American advisers on the ground, a few hundred million dollars in aid.

## TURMOIL IN THE SOUTH, CONSOLIDATION IN THE NORTH

And indeed, for a time after 1954, the gamble appeared to be paying off, at least on the surface. Diem moved swiftly to crush his internal opposition and began to consolidate his political position. He was helped by the exodus of almost one million Catholics from North to South who were said to have 'voted with their feet' for freedom. The real story was more complex. American officials, convinced that a massive migration out of the Vietminh-controlled North would prove a major embarrassment to Ho Chi Minh, were key players in the effort. Encouraged by the Catholic hierarchy and organized by Diem's US adviser Colonel Edward Lansdale and his team, entire parishes were moved south, many making the trip in American ships. Priests convinced the reluctant by informing them that 'Christ has gone to the South,' while Lansdale offered the incentives of five acres of land and a water buffalo. His agents also circulated stories of Vietminh concentration camps and the possibility of a US atomic bomb attack on the North.

Unquestionably, many of the migrants were deeply anti-communist and feared for their well-being in Ho Chi Minh's North. But there can also be no doubt that these tactics by the priests and by Lansdale were instrumental in convincing large numbers of others to come. Regardless, the campaign achieved its objective. Once settled in South Vietnam, this refugee population was a significant political asset to Diem, forming a substantial and dependent bloc of loyal voters. (By comparison, about 120,000 civilians migrated from South to North Vietnam.)

The notion that a 'flight to freedom' had occurred in Vietnam quickly took hold in the American popular consciousness. In a best-selling book titled *Deliver Us from Evil*, Lt. Tom Dooley, a US navy doctor who participated in the transportation of refugees, leveled horrific – and unsubstantiated – charges against the Hanoi regime for atrocities committed against those fleeing the 'Godless cruelties of Communism.' He also exaggerated his own and America's good works in the resulting 'Passage to Freedom.' And no one reading Dooley's book or watching the movie based on it could fail to see his plea for a full American commitment to help South Vietnam: 'We had come late to Vietnam, but we had come. And we brought not bombs and guns, but help and love' [94 *p. 58*].

Having consolidated his power base to a substantial degree, Diem in 1955 called for an election to determine whether the southern Vietnamese wanted a monarchy under Bao Dai or a republic under his own presidency. He did this because Bao Dai, who had close ties to religious sects opposed to Diem's rule, had ordered him to resign. Of the 6 million people who voted, 99 percent supported Diem. In Saigon he received 200,000 more votes than there were registered voters. The blatant election-rigging concerned American officials ('All you need is a fairly large majority,' Edward Lansdale had advised him beforehand, 'not 99.99 percent'), but they were sufficiently impressed with his performance to step up aid. Thus came into being the Republic of Vietnam (RVN). In the next two years there was talk of a 'Diem miracle' in South Vietnam, and US officials began making hopeful speeches about South Vietnam being a potential 'showcase' for America's foreign aid program. Diem's 1957 visit to the United States marked a high point in his leadership, as he was extravagantly praised by American political leaders and journalists for having achieved stability for South Vietnam and strong growth in the South's economy. He was accorded the honor of addressing Congress.

But appearances were deceptive. Even as he strengthened his position, Diem alienated key groups in South Vietnamese society with policies that favored the country's minority Catholic population, and with his refusal to follow through on a promised land reform program that might have won him peasant sympathies. In Long An province, for example, adjacent to Saigon, fewer than 1,000 of 35,000 tenants received property. Even worse, Diem antagonized peasants by requiring them to pay for land they had been given free by the Vietminh in the war against the French. Communists capitalized on this crude policy [1].

At the heart of Diem's problems was his very limited concept of political leadership. He lacked the ability to compromise, a shortcoming that became increasingly problematic as time went on. To neutralize the influence of Vietminh activists who remained in the South, the regime created 'agrovilles,' uprooting and resettling – and thereby further antagonizing – the peasantry. No less important, the American aid program, while essential to keeping South Vietnam alive, fostered a dependency rather than laying the foundation of a genuinely independent nation. American aid had built a castle on sand. Remove the US aid and the economy and military could swiftly collapse. Neither Diem nor his American benefactors gave much thought to the promotion of democracy or indeed to any political reform. When US officials on rare occasions did push for moves in that direction, the Saigon leader ignored them, suggesting the very real limits of Washington's influence (and, again, foreshadowing the 1960s). By the late 1950s, unrest in South Vietnam was rising rapidly [102].

These developments suggest that the Diem experiment may have been doomed even had his regime not faced such a formidable foe as Ho Chi Minh's North Vietnam. Ho's presence, however, made the odds even longer. The Hanoi leadership had moved cautiously in the period after the Geneva Conference with respect to the issue of unification. Well aware that neither Moscow nor Beijing supported an aggressive policy, since such might bring on a direct confrontation with Washington, it too sought to avoid giving the Americans any pretext to intervene. A Politburo resolution issued in early September 1954 ('The New Situation, the New Mission, and the New Policy of the Party') called for a shift from war to peace, from the struggle for reunification to building a new society. The resolution called for attempts in the South to try, by legal and illegal means, to consolidate peace and implement the Geneva Accords. This policy was affirmed at the Seventh Plenum of the Vietnamese Workers' Party (Lao Dong) Central Committee in March 1955: the delegates chose a policy of strengthening the DRV while waging a political struggle in South Vietnam and using diplomacy to gain support among progressive peoples elsewhere in the world [51].

In 1955, the Hanoi government launched a major land reform campaign under the control of cadres sent out by the central land reform committee. Careful party guidelines distinguished between rich peasants who were patriotic or traitorous, between productive and unproductive landlords, but these distinctions were increasingly ignored as the campaign became increasingly radicalized and gained a momentum of its own. Anxious to avoid indictment, peasants trumped up charges against their neighbors, while others accused their rivals of imaginary crimes. Anyone suspected of having worked for the French ran the risk of being executed as a 'traitor,' and other victims included those who had shown insufficient love for the Vietminh [133].

The government in Hanoi has never published an official count of those killed in the land reform, but thousands died. And thousands more were interned in forced labor camps. In August 1956, shortly after the campaign, Ho Chi Minh issued a public pronouncement that 'errors have been committed,' and he promised that those wrongly classified as landlords and rich peasants would be correctly reclassified. Other officials dutifully echoed his admission, disclosing that even loyal Vietminh veterans had been wrongly tried and executed.

Thousands of survivors were released and sent back to their villages amid exhortations to the nation to forgive and forget. But that proved difficult. Tensions continued. Victims took revenge against the cadres who had persecuted them. In several areas, peasants refused to obey directives, and North Vietnam foundered in an atmosphere of suspicion and apprehension. Describing the mood, the official Hanoi newspaper, *Nhan Dan*, wrote that 'brothers no longer dare to visit each other, and people dare not greet each other in the street.' The world, which was then focused on the Hungarian uprising against Soviet domination, paid no attention to the episode. But Ho, realizing that his reputation for moderation was at stake, introduced further liberal measures – conceding, however, that they were inadequate to repair the damage. Vo Nguyen Giap issued a similar *mea culpa*. 'We attacked on too large a front and, seeing enemies everywhere, resorted to terror, which became far too widespread. Worse still, torture came to be regarded as normal practice' [133].

With the end of these Agricultural Reform Tribunals, political life in North Vietnam settled down. It settled down to wait for the national elections called for in the Geneva Accords and scheduled for 1956. Hanoi officials were intent on reunification under their rule, but they hoped to do so not by bullets but by ballots, by way of an election victory.

Did party leaders in Hanoi really expect the elections to take place? This has long been a matter of debate, but it seems most likely that they did [53; 198]. They no doubt hoped that pressure from the Geneva Conference co-chairmen, Britain and the USSR, and other nations such as France, China, Canada, and India, would force Saigon and its American ally to hold the elections. In Britain and France, some officials clung for a long time to the hope that the elections would take place, and even in the United States there were observers who appeared to believe that some form of all-Vietnam vote would occur; it is hard to believe Hanoi would not learn of these sentiments. When Diem in the summer of 1955 refused to hold even the consultations called for at Geneva, DRV leaders were disappointed.

They were not, however, prepared to alter their two-pronged strategy of consolidating power in the North while working toward reunification with the South. Vietminh officials in the South began exerting pressure on Hanoi to work harder for the second objective. In 1956 Le Duan, the senior Communist leader in the South, issued a lengthy report, 'The Path to Revolution in the South,' which called for the southern cadres to prepare for a long-term political struggle while also suggesting to the North that the time might come for military action [21]. Hanoi responded cautiously. Ho and his colleagues were fully engaged in nation-building in the North and had no desire to provoke the United States, especially given the continued lack of support for rapid reunification of Vietnam from the Soviet Union and China. The Moscow government under Nikita Khrushchev promoted 'peaceful co-existence' with the West; China, absorbed with its own national development, had no desire for another Korea-style war against the United States. The Soviets even went so far as to propose in 1957 that both Vietnams, North and South, be admitted to the United Nations, which would acknowledge a more or less permanent partition of the country.

Over time, however, Hanoi's leaders gradually shifted their position and opted to encourage and support the insurgency taking shape in the South. The key decisions came in 1959. Recognizing that the revolutionaries in the South were desperate for help and also that Diem's oppressiveness had created a favorable atmosphere for revolution, the party in the spring of 1959 authorized the resumption of armed struggle and took active measures to support it. Among other things, the leadership established a special task force to create what soon would be known worldwide as the Ho Chi Minh Trail, an infiltration route of several hundred miles to move men and supplies into South Vietnam through Laos. The Trail's segments gradually were widened, and bicycles were introduced to transport supplies. With strengthened frames, the bicycles could handle loads of 220 to 330 pounds each, though occasional loads of more than 700 pounds were reported. En route, infiltrators typically averaged six miles a day, meaning they took more than a month to reach South Vietnam.

Hanoi also sent back to the South many Vietminh who had come North after Geneva and instructed them to use force to protect themselves and to work to undermine the Saigon government. In September 1960, the

Third Party Congress of the Vietnamese Workers' Party formally approved armed struggle, assigning liberation of the South equal priority with consolidation of the North. And in December 1960, at Hanoi's direction, southern revolutionaries founded the National Front for the Liberation of South Vietnam (NLF), a broad-based organization led by communists but designed to rally all those disaffected by Diem by promising sweeping reforms and the establishment of genuine independence [*Doc. 10*] [53].

Herein lies one of the core issues for later arguments over how to assign responsibility for the Vietnam War. Did the insurgency that gained momentum in South Vietnam in 1959–60 come about because of the actions of southern insurgents, with little or no involvement by the North, or was the formation of the NLF the opening stage of an armed attack from Hanoi? In other words, was this at root a civil war between two mutually hostile indigenous groups in the South or a war of external aggression? Conflicting answers to this question would in later years cause deep divisions in the United States and indeed in any number of other countries where the war was debated. Critics of US involvement tended to argue passionately in favor of the former, that it was a civil war launched over Hanoi's strong reservations; American officials and their supporters would speak with equal vehemence for the position that this was from the start a war against South Vietnam ordered by and directed from Hanoi.

Who was right? Neither, and both. Hanoi, it seems clear, played an active role in the escalation of the struggle in the South; without that involvement, southern insurgents would almost certainly have been unable to defeat a Saigon government receiving American assistance. Yet there is no doubt that opposition in the South to the Saigon government ran deep, without which no amount of pressure from the DRV could have brought the situation in South Vietnam to the point of revolution. As one scholar has summarized it, it was 'an insurgent movement inspired by local conditions in the south but guided and directed from Hanoi' [194; 53 p. 137].

For some observers, the debate over the North's role in the insurgency in the South is meaningless, since the Geneva Accords had unambiguously affirmed that Vietnam was legally one nation, albeit one to be temporarily divided at the seventeenth parallel. When the Diem regime refused to hold consultations on elections for reunification, so the argument goes, Hanoi was absolved from any responsibility to abide by the terms of the agreement. To DRV leaders, Vietnam remained one country, and any measures taken to bring about reunification of the two halves were in the end justifiable.

Whatever one's position on this question, one thing is incontrovertible: by the end of 1960, an insurgency of major proportions was under way in South Vietnam. Ngo Dinh Diem's Republic of Vietnam was about to face its toughest test. And in Washington, a new administration prepared to take power.

# CHAPTER FOUR

# THE CRISIS DEEPENS

John F. Kennedy's role in the Vietnam War remains the most controversial aspect of his public image and record. This is partly because important policy decisions were enacted during his one thousand days in the White House, and partly because his death by an assassin's bullet in November 1963 followed so closely on the heels of the ouster of Ngo Dinh Diem in a US-sponsored *coup d'état*. But there is also something else that fuels the controversy: namely, the suddenness of his death. Many supporters of Kennedy believe he intended at the time of his death to withdraw from Vietnam, either in the immediate short term or following the 1964 election. The most well known recent proponent of this view is film-maker Oliver Stone, whose motion picture *JFK* went so far as to suggest that Kennedy's determination on this score helped bring on his death.

The chief objective of these Kennedy admirers is not difficult to discern: they wish to shield Kennedy from the débâcle in Southeast Asia. And indeed, Kennedy's record in Vietnam was sufficiently ambiguous and complex to allow for such an interpretation, to convince even many independent observers that he would have taken a different path from that of his successor. It was a record marked by repeated rejections of opportunities to pursue a political solution to the conflict; by a major expansion of the American presence in Vietnam, thus violating the limits prescribed in the Geneva Accords; but also, and no less important, by numerous presidential vetoes of plans for a still-larger American commitment to the war [84; 123; 165].

The men Kennedy chose to be his chief foreign policy advisers would be key figures in decision-making on Vietnam, both before his death and after. An impressive trio they were. To head the State Department, Kennedy chose Dean Rusk, a former Rhodes scholar and president of the Rockefeller Foundation. Robert McNamara, former professor at the Harvard Business School, left his job as president of Ford Motor Company to become secretary of defense, while McGeorge Bundy, a 41-year-old dean at Harvard, was selected to become Kennedy's special assistant for National Security Affairs [16; 176]. For the next four years, as Vietnam gradually became America's top foreign policy concern, these three men would be at the center of policy, until in 1965 they helped make Vietnam a full-scale American war. Throughout those four years, the three would advise against seeking a diplomatic solution to the conflict (though McNamara toward the end was more open to the idea than the other two).

The first substantial efforts at shifting the struggle in Vietnam from the battlefield to the negotiating table came, not surprisingly, after Kennedy agreed to just such a shift in Laos, the narrow, landlocked nation situated between Thailand and Vietnam. The post-1954 infusion of American aid and advisory personnel had not solidified pro-Western rule in that nation, and by the start of 1961 the US-sponsored government of Phoumi Nosavan faced imminent defeat at the hands of the communist-backed Pathet Lao. Dwight Eisenhower, in a meeting the day before Kennedy's January inauguration, stressed the strategic importance of Laos, calling it the key to all of Southeast Asia and apparently warning JFK that if it fell the United States would have to 'write off the whole area.' He professed a desire for a negotiated settlement, but expressly ruled out neutralization. 'It would be fatal,' Eisenhower told Kennedy, 'for us to permit Communists to insert themselves into the Laotian government' [*Doc. 11*] [30].

In the months that followed, several of Kennedy's top advisers echoed Eisenhower's sense of alarm and recommended military intervention, but JFK never authorized it. He developed strong doubts about the intrinsic importance of Laos to US security. He worried about its difficult geography; about the likely lack of public support for a long-term commitment; about the lack of an 'exit strategy' for any such commitment. By the early spring he had made up his mind: he would pursue a diplomatic solution, even if domestic critics would brand him an 'appeaser' for doing so [54].

America's chief allies had something to do with the decision. They believed that the West's stake in Laos was small, almost non-existent. On a spring 1961 visit to the United States, British Prime Minister Harold Macmillan cautioned Kennedy against a deeper US commitment to a place that was militarily indefensible and not vital to Western security. During a discussion held on a yacht cruise down the Potomac River, Macmillan refused to commit precious British resources to Laos, especially in defense of a military that had not distinguished itself in fighting; when the yacht passed a local college team rowing a racing scull down the river, the prime minister asked: 'What have we here? The Laotian navy?' [96].

France also questioned the idea of a concerted effort to ensure a pro-Western Laos. When Kennedy visited Paris in May, de Gaulle told him that France would not support a Western military intervention in that country. The French experience in the region had made clear that military action could never achieve lasting results, and therefore the best solution to the Laos problem was neutralization. Kennedy responded that at least the threat of American military intervention might be necessary, but de Gaulle disagreed. 'For you, intervention in this region will be an entanglement without end,' he said. Nationalism would always prove stronger than any foreign power, as the French experience had shown. The Frenchman's words apparently made an impression on Kennedy. When General Maxwell D. Taylor and Walt W. Rostow of the National Security Council staff urged him to intervene with US forces if the communists renewed their Laotian offensive, Kennedy reportedly balked, replying that de Gaulle had 'spoken with feeling of the difficulty of fighting in this part of the world' [121; 124].

Kennedy thus chose to spurn Eisenhower's advice and sidestep Laos. In May he informed London that the United States would back a joint Soviet–British initiative to convene a Geneva conference on Laos for the purpose of negotiating a settlement among the communists, neutralists, and American-supported military that were contending for power in the country. Kennedy assigned the seasoned negotiator W. Averell Harriman as the US representative. The thirteen months of negotiations that followed brought forth a consensus that the only compromise with any chance of success was one wherein the pro-communist Pathet Lao and the neutralist faction were given positions reasonably commensurate with their actual power. The final agreement, signed in July 1962, created a 'neutral and independent' Laos, led by a coalition government under the neutralist prime minister Souvanna Phouma but in which the Pathet Lao shared power.

The realities of the situation in Laos made an attempt at a negotiated settlement the only feasible choice, but by adopting this solution Kennedy knew he was opening himself to Republican charges that he was 'losing' Southeast Asia just as Truman had 'lost' China. He felt confident that the administration was pursuing the best available course, but feared that a Laos agreement giving the Pathet Lao a share of power would be branded a second defeat (after the Bay of Pigs débâcle earlier in 1961, in which a group of US-trained and equipped Cuban exiles tried to overthrow the government of Fidel Castro) in the face of communist power. A third such defeat could be politically devastating, Kennedy believed, as he made clear to the US ambassador to India, John Kenneth Galbraith: 'There are just so many concessions that one can make to communists in one year and survive politically ... We just can't have another defeat this year in Vietnam' [107 *p. 474*].

But it was not just the domestic political implications that concerned Kennedy; international factors were also important. Kennedy perceived the Laotian civil war as part of the larger Cold War struggle, and he saw Nikita Khrushchev's January 1961 speech in support of wars of national liberation as essentially a challenge to the United States rather than primarily a response to China's claim to be the true champion of Third World revolutionaries. Khrushchev added to Kennedy's uneasiness in 1961 by stepping up Soviet airlifts to insurgents in Laos and the Congo and by increasing aid to Castro's Cuba and to North Vietnam. As if that were not enough, Khrushchev also threatened to resume the Berlin blockade. In October, just before the Berlin crisis ended, Kennedy told Arthur Krock of the *New York Times* that 'it was a hell of a note ... that he had to try to handle the Berlin situation with the Communists encouraging foreign aggressors all over the place ... in Viet-Nam, Laos, etc.'

The Laos agreement thus served only to incline Kennedy and his principal advisers toward a military solution and away from a negotiated settlement in Vietnam – at least for the foreseeable future. They soon began to militarize the direct American intervention that Eisenhower had initiated. Eisenhower had been willing to breach the political elements of the 1954 Geneva settlement almost as soon as they were agreed, but he largely abided by the military stipulations, even to the extent of limiting the number of American advisers to the 685 prescribed at Geneva. Kennedy had fewer reservations about violating many of Geneva's key military provisions, and by the time of his assassination the number of US military advisers in Vietnam numbered more than 16,000. Many were assigned to accompany, and sometimes actually to lead, South Vietnamese troops into combat. To be sure, Kennedy resisted pressures from the US military and many of his senior civilian advisers for the introduction of American ground troop units into Vietnam, and he continued to do so throughout his term in office. Nevertheless, he did establish a substantial military presence in Vietnam, and in so doing commenced a process that narrowed his options and those of his successor.

Of course, Kennedy and his advisers claimed, at the time and later, that their options were narrowed already in 1961. Secretary of State Dean Rusk represented the administration's view when he told Andrei Gromyko during the Laos negotiations that both the Soviets and the North Vietnamese should never forget that the United States was 'deeply committed to South Vietnam and cannot and will not accept its destruction.' In reality, however, the Eisenhower administration had not formally committed Kennedy to defend South Vietnam. The SEATO treaty, as we have seen, required only that member nations consult with one another. Furthermore, Eisenhower had in October 1954 made clear that a large US aid program to South Vietnam was dependent on the Diem government 'undertaking needed reforms' and generally acting to further South Vietnamese democracy. By 1960–61, many in Saigon, including Elbridge Durbrow, the US ambassador, argued that those requirements had not been met. Eisenhower's policy toward South Vietnam left Kennedy with options other than to support a Diemist regime, but he was determined to keep South Vietnam out of communist hands. He saw Diem as the best vehicle by which to do so.

## THE FALL 1961 DECISIONS

And so Kennedy chose, as Jean Lacouture has written, 'to separate the two Indochinese problems, to make peace in Laos while trying to win the war in Vietnam' [116 *p. 83*]. In May 1961 he accepted the recommendation of a special task force to increase the size of the Saigon regime's army (ARVN) by 20,000 men, and to send an additional 100 American advisers to Vietnam, making a total of nearly 800. More would come in the summer. The measures did little to help the situation on the ground. By the fall of that year, the Diem regime was in deep trouble. NLF recruitment jumped dramatically in the summer, and in the early autumn the Vietcong (as the NLF's military guerrillas were popularly known) drastically stepped up their operations. Before long they had seized control of villages in many regions of South Vietnam. The result was increased political turmoil in South Vietnam, and it came as no surprise when in September Diem urgently requested additional economic assistance. By early October, both the Joint Chiefs of Staff (JCS) and the NSC were leaning toward the introduction of sizable American combat forces into Vietnam.

Kennedy remained skeptical. He had no desire to send American troops to the Asian mainland. Already in 1954 he had warned against following such a course, and he had stuck to that position ever since. Now, to a group of reporters he expressed grave doubt that the United States should interfere in 'civil disturbances' caused by guerrillas, adding that 'it was hard to prove that this wasn't largely the situation in Vietnam.' This was Kennedy's dilemma: he did not want to expand the American military commitment, but he feared a continued military and political deterioration in South Vietnam. In October he sent a team headed by his personal military adviser General Maxwell D. Taylor to Vietnam to get a first-hand look at the war and consider US options, including the sending of combat forces [91; 144]

The Taylor mission was to be one of the most important such missions of the entire Kennedy period, and its findings energized both the proponents and opponents of an increased American military commitment in Vietnam. The key members of the mission were Taylor and White House adviser Walt Rostow, both of whom had made no secret of their hawkishness on the war. During a two-week tour they found a desperate political and military situation in South Vietnam, and they recommended a series of measures that the United States should take to prevent further deterioration. Specifically, the president should authorize the training and equipping of the Civil Guard and the Self-Defense Corps to relieve the regular South Vietnamese army of static assignments, and dispatch considerably more American helicopters and light aviation to increase the mobility of ARVN units for offensive operations.

Most important, in an 'eyes only' memorandum to Kennedy, Taylor proposed the dispatch of an 8,000-man military task force to South Vietnam. The stated purpose of the unit would be to assist in repairing the extensive damage caused by flooding in the Mekong Delta. But under the cloak provided by the humanitarian activity of engineers and medics, American infantrymen would conduct combat operations against the Vietcong. Taylor argued that the presence of American troops would raise morale in South Vietnam and demonstrate the resolve of the United States to resist communism in Southeast Asia [*Doc. 12*] [143].

In Washington, Secretary of Defense McNamara and the JCS rejected Taylor's proposal as inadequate. The expedition of only 8,000 US combat troops to Vietnam, they said, 'probably will not tip the scales decisively [and] we would be almost certain to get increasingly mired down in an inclusive struggle.' To show that 'we mean business,' they urged the deployment of six US divisions – some 200,000 men. The NSC's Robert Komer also argued for an immediate, decisive military commitment. 'True,' Komer wrote, 'we may end up with something approaching another Korea, but I think the best way of avoiding this is to move fast now before the war spreads to the extent that a Korean type commitment is required' [219].

Not all voices were so belligerent. Indeed, in this important period Kennedy received a rather broad range of options from his advisers. In an 11 November personal memorandum to Kennedy, chief Laos negotiator Harriman (soon to become assistant secretary of state for far eastern affairs) urged a diplomatic settlement for Vietnam based on the 1954 Geneva Accords, arguing that the Diem regime was 'repressive, dictatorial, and unpopular.' Harriman argued that the Soviet Union was interested in stabilizing the Southeast Asian situation, and suggested that the United States agree to reduce its military presence in South Vietnam as peace was restored in the area. For their part, the North Vietnamese and the NLF would agree to a cease-fire, accept a strong United Nations Control Commission, and achieve eventual reunification, possibly through elections. The United States should not, Harriman concluded, 'stake its prestige in Vietnam,' a point also made to Kennedy by John Kenneth Galbraith [67; 121].

The undersecretary of state, Chester Bowles, was even more adamant. For months he had urged Kennedy to consider the expansion of the Laos neutralization to include all of Southeast Asia, and he was convinced that if adopted, the Taylor recommendations would lead the United States 'full blast up a dead end street,' and 'constitute a long step toward a full-blown war of unpredictable dimensions.' Similarly, Abram Chayes, the State Department's legal adviser, attacked the Taylor proposal for focusing principally on 'military and semi-military means,' and he advised Kennedy to seek a negotiated settlement [20].

George Ball, assistant secretary of state for economic affairs and soon to replace Bowles as undersecretary, met with Kennedy on 7 November and predicted that the Taylor report, if implemented, would produce 'the most tragic of circumstances.' Ball asserted that the Vietnamese topography was 'totally unsuitable for the commitment of American forces,' and argued that American prestige was sure to suffer if the United States became too deeply committed. Speaking of the Taylor plan, Ball added prophetically: 'If we go down that road, we might have, within five years, 300,000 men in the rice paddies and the jungles of Vietnam and never be able to find them.' In sum, the Taylor proposal was 'an open-ended commitment of people' that was based on ideas that were 'absurd.' Ball told Kennedy he 'had better be damned careful' [4 *p. 410*].

But Ball and the other advocates of negotiations were hemmed in. Though each managed to make their misgivings known to Kennedy, they understood that the president's inner circle was at the time asking not *whether* but *how* to commit US resources. Both Robert McNamara and McGeorge Bundy advocated an increased American commitment to en-suring the survival of a non-communist South Vietnamese regime, with US ground troops if necessary. Dean Rusk was more reluctant about deploying such troops and even cautioned against making 'a major commitment [of] American prestige to a losing horse.' But he too favored standing firm in Vietnam and argued against initiating negotiations. Most important, Kennedy himself was skeptical of such a course. Upon hearing Ball's 7 November prediction that Vietnam might one day demand 300,000 US troops, he laughed and said: 'Well, George, you're supposed to be one of the smartest guys in town, but you're crazier than hell. That will never happen' [ibid.].

## THE CREDIBILITY IMPERATIVE

The advocates of a negotiated settlement thus operated from a severe dis-advantage. They represented, as the State Department's Abram Chayes later said, 'all the non-power in the Department,' with the result that 'it just never flew' [219 *p. 81*]. Still mindful of the setbacks in the Bay of Pigs and at Vienna and nervous about conservative criticism of the Laos negotiations and the handling of the Berlin crisis, Kennedy and his advisers worried about how this could influence administration promises to wage the Cold War vigorously. After leaving office Eisenhower had vowed to keep a close eye on Kennedy's foreign policy, and throughout 1961 Republicans and right-wing Democrats had charged the administration with weakness and vacil-lation. Kennedy feared that a decision to negotiate on Vietnam would harm his credibility and provoke a domestic political attack similar to that which Harry Truman had to endure after the 'fall of China' a dozen years earlier.

But it was not just the domestic dimension of credibility that concerned Kennedy. Perhaps more important in his thinking was Vietnam's potential impact on America's international position. Kennedy deemed it essential to demonstrate the credibility of America's commitments, to convince adversaries and allies alike of American firmness, determination, and dependability. The moves the United States now made, Kennedy told Rusk and McNamara in mid-November, would be 'examined on both sides of the Iron Curtain ... as a measure of the administration's intentions and determination,' and if it chose to negotiate it might 'in fact be judged weaker than in Laos' and cause 'a major crisis of nerve' throughout Southeast Asia. Similarly, a Rusk–McNamara report warned the same month that 'The loss of South Viet-Nam would ... undermine the credibility of American commitments elsewhere' [130].

The 'doctrine of credibility' had by the fall of 1961 supplanted the domino theory in American thinking on Vietnam, or at least altered the way that theory was conceived. Kennedy administration officials were less concerned than their predecessors had been that each nation that fell to communism would endanger its immediate neighbor; they were less attached, that is, to the notion of what one might call a 'territorial domino theory.' Instead, Kennedy and his advisers adhered to what Jonathan Schell among others has called a 'psychological domino theory'; they feared the impact of one nation's fall on other nations the world over which, by merely watching the spectacle, would lose confidence in the power of the United States. 'In this thinking,' Schell has written, 'Vietnam became a "test case" of the United States' will to use its power in world affairs. 'If the United States could not muster the "determination" to prevail in Vietnam, it was believed, then it would be showing, once and for all, that it lacked the determination to prevail in any conflict anywhere' [169 *pp. 9–10*].

If Kennedy refused to negotiate on Vietnam in the fall of 1961, he also refused to go as far as the Taylor report suggested. He did approve increased financial and military aid to the Diem regime, and he authorized the dispatch of two fully armed helicopter companies and an increased number of American military advisers. But he also accepted the arguments of advisers such as Rusk (and McNamara, who had backed away from his agreement with the Chiefs) that the deployment of combat troops could effectively ruin the Laos negotiations and perhaps lead to an escalated war in Vietnam itself. The advisers also cautioned the president that should the proposed 8,000 troops be fired upon, Washington would be confronted with a more difficult choice: to send in additional troops or withdraw completely. 'If we commit 6–8,000 troops and then pull them out when the going gets rough we will be finished in Vietnam and probably all of Southeast Asia,' one NSC staff member warned. The president agreed. For the moment at least, there would be no fighting troops.

With these November 1961 decisions, then, Kennedy rejected the alternatives of negotiating a peace settlement or deploying combat forces and chose instead a down-the-middle approach of increased aid and advisers. He understood that these steps by themselves were not enough to save South Vietnam, but he chose them because they bought him time: they left him free to expand or contract the US military commitment. What he perhaps did not understand was that even a relatively modest increase in the American commitment to South Vietnam served to make any such contraction more difficult. By raising the number of American advisers to 3,000 (more than four times the level authorized by the Geneva Accords), and by authorizing them to take part in combat operations, Kennedy had increased America's stake in Vietnam.

FLEETING GAINS: 1962

For a time, the strategy appeared to pay off. The infusion of American aid and advisers in late 1961 yielded immediate if temporary results in the war against the Vietcong. The helicopters dramatically increased the mobility of Diem's troops, allowing them to leapfrog and surround NLF military detachments. The use of napalm, a jellied gasoline that burns deeply into the skin, also brought results. General Paul Harkins, head of the Military Assistance Command, Vietnam (MACV), exulted that napalm 'really puts the fear of God into the Viet Cong ... and that is what counts.'

The administration also made much of the 'strategic hamlet' program, which had been suggested to Diem by British counter-insurgency expert Robert G. K. Thompson and was designed to insulate and protect the peasantry from the Vietcong. The idea was straightforward: if the Vietcong were denied access to villages on which they depended for food, intelligence, and recruits, they would be denied the capability of waging war. And just how would this access be denied? Through the relocation of entire villages into supposedly secure areas where the Saigon government would provide food, housing, and various educational and other social services. As a result, so the argument went, the peasant would come to see the South Vietnamese government as a friendly and capable force. Diem, aware of his government's lack of support in the countryside, embraced the Thompson plan and placed his brother Ngo Dinh Nhu in charge of overseeing the construction of the hamlets.

It all looked quite promising, and the first half of 1962 witnessed numerous public and private expressions of confidence on the part of senior US officials that the war was on the way to being won. The optimism proved unfounded. Militarily, the ARVN may have seized the initiative, but it meant little, as Vietcong bases remained almost impossible to locate amidst the dense forests and swampy paddylands of South Vietnam. Very often, guerrillas would simply wait for government troops to withdraw from conquered territory and then reoccupy it. More important, the 1962

American–Diem military offensive did nothing to stem the political revolution against the Saigon regime taking place in the countryside. The strategic hamlet program served only to alienate peasants from the Diem regime – most people resented being moved from lands their families had lived on for generations. Few of the hamlets had much in the way of social services, and few were secure from enemy infiltration. Many were oddly lacking in young men, who had already joined the Vietcong. Moreover, funds that were supposed to provide for the peasantry all too often went into the pockets of Diem's officials. More and more peasants refused to pay land taxes and many chose to back the NLF, with its aggressive land reform platform and anti-Diem line.

These fundamental problems in the war effort were not lost on the advocates of American disengagement. Several mid-level US officials, among them Chester Bowles and John Kenneth Galbraith, said Diem was a lost cause and urged Kennedy to give serious consideration to pursuing a political settlement, but they encountered stiff opposition. The JCS warned that 'any reversal of U.S. policy could have disastrous effects, not only on our relationship with South Vietnam, but with the rest of our Asian and other allies as well.' They reminded McNamara of Kennedy's frequent reiterations of America's determination to stand tough against the Vietcong, and urged that 'the present U.S. policy toward South Vietnam, as announced by the president, should be pursued vigorously to a successful conclusion.' McNamara needed no convincing, and his fellow senior advisers, McGeorge Bundy and Dean Rusk, likewise continued to argue for persisting in the war effort [136].

Kennedy was more skeptical, and he continued in 1962 to exhibit the same contradictory impulses on Vietnam that had been on such stark display in 1961. On the one hand, he told Averell Harriman and NSC staffer Michael Forrestal that he sympathized with Galbraith's concerns, and that the United States should 'be prepared to seize upon any favorable moment to reduce our commitment, recognizing that the moment might yet be some time away.' On the other hand, he told Dean Rusk privately and American journalists publicly that the United States must not tire of its commitment to South Vietnam. It appears that for a time, at least, he thought he could reconcile those seemingly contradictory objectives – that he could achieve, in other words, an acceptable settlement that would guarantee the preservation of a non-communist South Vietnam and also allow the United States to withdraw. JFK's optimism was sufficiently strong that in July he asked McNamara to initiate plans for a phased withdrawal of US advisers from South Vietnam, but he did so based on indications of success emanating from Saigon. The plan, made operational in July 1962, called for the phased withdrawals to begin at the end of 1963 and continue for several years – *provided* the war was going well.

Throughout the summer and into the fall, American officials in Saigon continued to paint a rosy picture of the war effort. In particular, General Harkins, who was famous for insisting on favorable reports from his officers, sent back detailed reports purporting to show success after success in operations against the Vietcong. Harkins was convinced that the answer to the insurgency was essentially military, not political, something that no doubt goes a long to explain his optimism – militarily, the war did go relatively well through the end of 1962, though the Vietcong continued to evade major engagements and gradually became adept at shooting down the all-important helicopters. On the political front, however, the front that involved winning the 'hearts and minds' of the South Vietnamese people, the autumn saw continued NLF gains.

The Front's dominant position was made crystal clear in January 1963, in a major battle between Vietcong companies and the ARVN near the village of Ap Bac. An American adviser, the legendary Lt. Col John Paul Vann, urged his ARVN division commander to attack the guerrillas concentrated near the village. Vann got his wish, but the results were very different from what he expected. Despite outnumbering enemy forces 10 to 1 and enjoying overwhelming advantages in weaponry, the ARVN refused to take the initiative in the fighting, and would not leave the protection of their armored personnel carriers. The battle ended ingloriously, with ARVN forces firing on each other and the guerrillas escaping. The South Vietnamese forces counted 61 dead and 100 wounded, while the Vietcong suffered only three deaths.

For many of the American journalists in South Vietnam, Ap Bac confirmed something they had been suspecting for months: that the war effort was in fact going poorly. Young reporters such as Neil Sheehan of United Press International and David Halberstam of the *New York Times*, though still supportive of the aims of US policy, had since the fall of 1962 become increasingly skeptical of the optimistic claims emanating from Harkins's headquarters; now the ARVN had suffered a crushing defeat at the hands of a much smaller force. It raised very large questions about the state of the war effort and about official claims concerning that war effort, questions that would henceforth appear with more and more frequency in America's newspapers [177].

## SUMMER OF DISCONTENT

If Kennedy had been looking for a face-saving and domestically defensible way out of Vietnam, Diem and his brother Ngo Dinh Nhu presented it to him during the spring and summer of 1963 with a series of attacks on the Buddhists. From the outset of his rule Diem had regarded the Catholic refugees from North Vietnam as the core of his constituency, and his regime had effectively denied Buddhists – who comprised over 80 percent of the population – equal access to employment and government services. Buddhist agitation had risen steadily in 1962–63, and it erupted full-blown on 8 May 1963 when Diem's troops fired into a crowd of Buddhists who were celebrating Buddha's birthday by waving religious flags, thereby violating the regime's rule that forbade the exhibit of any banner but the government's. In the major South Vietnamese cities in the weeks that followed, students took to the streets to support Buddhist charges of religious discrimination. Nhu, increasingly powerful in the government and the mastermind behind the May crackdown, countered with raids on pagodas, mass arrests, and martial law, each of which provoked more marches and self-immolations. It was a cycle that would repeat itself again and again in the months that followed.

American officials were perplexed and irritated at Nhu's repressive actions, and at Diem's silent acquiescence. Their anger increased when Nhu's glamorous wife, Madame Nhu, publicly and with apparent glee dismissed the immolations as 'barbecues' and offered to supply the gasoline and matches for more. Nor was it merely Nhu's brutal tactics *vis-à-vis* the Buddhists that concerned American analysts. Equally worrisome were the reports that he might be contemplating seeking a deal with the Hanoi government. For several months Nhu had complained on occasion that there were too many Americans in South Vietnam, that Americans could never understand the Vietnamese way of life, and that it would be better if half the Americans in the South went home. In July and August 1963 he repeated these claims and told several people that he had commenced contacts with representatives of the DRV.

On 10 August, for example, in talks with British diplomats, Nhu spoke of having regular meetings with members of the 'Dien Bien Phu' generation in North Vietnam. There was a considerable body of patriotic individuals in Hanoi who were nationalists first and communists second, Nhu said, men who were in their mid-forties and who had fought against the French and who naturally had been in the ranks of Ho Chi Minh's forces because he had provided the power and organization to bring about the liberation. They were persons who rightly sought a Vietnamese solution to the Vietnamese problem and, Nhu added, 'I have had some of them sitting in this room' [121; 125].

Nhu's claims regarding the existence of North–South contacts take on added credibility when one considers that it was in North Vietnam's interest to explore the thinking of the *de facto* leader of the southern regime. The available evidence suggests strongly that Hanoi leaders in this period were broadly sympathetic to a negotiated settlement of the conflict. At several points in 1962 and early 1963, in fact, northern officials had expressed hopes for a settlement.

Why? They appear to have reasoned that, although Washington was more committed to the Vietnam conflict than to the one in Laos, the administration was reluctant to intervene directly in the struggle against the Vietcong. Kennedy might therefore be willing to accept a diplomatic solution, even if it were really a disguised defeat. Such a solution would allow Hanoi to meet one of its core aims – to avoid a direct military confrontation with the United States – and satisfy demands from both Beijing and Moscow that the Indochina conflict not be allowed to get out of hand. In July 1962, senior Politburo member Le Duan accordingly instructed the leadership of the southern resistance to avoid a major escalation of the war by keeping the fighting confined to the mountain and rural areas of South Vietnam (direct attacks on the cities could result in the Americans intervening directly in the war) and to work for a negotiated settlement and a US withdrawal [21; 51].

Even as they wished for a political settlement, however, Hanoi officials were not prepared to work actively for one. By mid-1963 they could take satisfaction in the growing success of the insurgency in the South, and the mounting problems of the Diem regime. Moreover, they did not want to alienate their powerful northern neighbor, China, by appearing too willing to reach an accommodation with a US-sponsored Saigon regime. More often than not, North Vietnamese public statements in 1963 echoed the Chinese position in the Sino-Soviet dispute – that is, as good Marxist-Leninists they claimed that the USSR under Nikita Khrushchev had deviated from pure doctrine in supporting 'revisionism' in Yugoslavia and in espousing 'peaceful co-existence' and 'world peace.'

GIVE PEACE A CHANCE?

As it happened, this desire for a diplomatic settlement combined with an unwillingness to work hard for one characterized the approach not only of the Hanoi leadership but also several other key world players. The French president, Charles de Gaulle, was the most outspoken in favor of a political solution among world leaders, and on 29 August he publicly called for a reunified Vietnam free of 'outside interference.' But de Gaulle cannot be considered an agitator for negotiations in this period; he was content to criticize US involvement, and predict its failure, without making explicit proposals for a settlement. Soviet and British officials shared de Gaulle's dim view of America's prospects in Vietnam, but were less willing to say so; like him, they were content to take a wait and see attitude [121].

Indeed, the USSR and Britain shared a very similar and very vexing dilemma, one they were never able to surmount in the critical two years that followed: how to affirm support for their respective allies in the war while also preventing a major conflagration. The Soviet government had traditionally favored negotiated settlements in East Asia. Its leaders were convinced that a major conflict would serve only to increase American and Chinese involvement in the region – eventualities to be avoided if at all possible. Yet Moscow officials also felt compelled to move warily, in large part because of the deepening of the Sino-Soviet split that occurred in the middle months of 1963. Should they appear too eager for a settlement, Soviet leaders knew, Beijing would accuse them of seeking 'peaceful co-existence' with the West at the expense of Hanoi and would claim leadership of the world revolutionary movement.

As for the British government of Harold Macmillan, its desire for a political solution in Indochina was outweighed by its desire to preserve good relations with the United States. American economic assistance had become steadily more important to London's financial officers in recent years, and there were a whole range of other bilateral issues perceived by the British to be more important than easing the turmoil in Indochina. On Vietnam, London was prepared to follow Washington's lead. The Macmillan government in fact had an agreement with Washington to avoid working for a negotiated solution until the war was clearly on the path to being won. 'The policy which we have agreed with the Americans is to avoid international discussion on Vietnam until the military situation has been restored,' F. A. Warner wrote in mid-1962, succinctly summarizing the British position [46; 121].

China, too, adhered to a low-key posture on Vietnam in 1963, albeit one tilted more strongly against early negotiations. In 1962, Beijing leaders had expressed explicit support for an international meeting on the war, but as the Sino-Soviet split deepened in 1963, and as the Diem regime faltered, their position hardened. In March and again in May 1963, high-level Chinese delegations visited Hanoi and pledged to officials there that if the war expanded to North Vietnam they could count on China as the strategic rear. In late August Chinese leader Mao Zedong received a delegation representing the NLF and issued a statement proclaiming support for its cause [29].

Does this mean Beijing authorities had renounced the idea of a great-power meeting on the war? Not necessarily. Since 1954 these officials had advised Hanoi to avoid a dramatic escalation of the war, and they were no less anxious than the North Vietnamese and the Soviets to avoid a direct military confrontation with the United States. They were careful, both at this point and in 1964, to avoid making specific pledges of support to the DRV in the event of an expanded war. They also avoided specifically ruling out a negotiated settlement, and it may be, as Southeast Asian specialists in the British Foreign Office surmised, that Beijing in the summer of 1963 still saw its cause being forwarded by a conference.

Not so the United States. In 1963, the Kennedy administration opposed any move to bring about an early diplomatic settlement, as it had since it came into office and as its predecessor had done before that. The mantra remained the same: the insurgency has to be defeated; no diplomacy can be undertaken until that result is assured. In other words, negotiations should be entered into only when the US/RVN side could dictate the terms. Note here that American officials were not merely skeptical of what negotiations might bring; they were downright fearful of the likely results. Far from merely hoping that a meeting would not be convened, they actively sought to prevent such a result. Hence the pressure they applied on London to work to that end. This American fear of early negotiations, which would become stronger in late 1963 and 1964, is in itself indirect but powerful additional evidence of their viability. Washington strategists fretted about negotiations on Vietnam precisely because they recognized that diplomacy represented a viable – if from their perspective also odious – means to bring the conflict to an end.

Here, then, are the two reasons why no negotiated settlement was close to being realized in mid-1963, despite the sympathy for such a solution in much of the world community: first, the proponents of a settlement were not willing to work hard for one; and second, the most important player of all, the United States, was resolutely opposed to an early deal. The Buddhist uprisings were an unmistakable symptom of the unraveling of the South Vietnamese social fabric, and they received heavy play in the American press. They gave Kennedy an avenue for disengagement that risked considerably less domestic political damage than ever before; he could have claimed that Diem and Nhu had flagrantly violated the stipulations for aid laid down by Eisenhower in 1954. But he chose not to do so, despite the failure of repeated American attempts to get Diem to compromise with the Buddhists, and despite growing evidence that the NLF was winning the war in the countryside.

Instead, Kennedy chose to continue America's involvement in the conflict. Rather than using the public outrage at the actions of Diem and Nhu as a plausible excuse for disengaging the United States from Vietnam, he opted to stay the course by, if necessary, replacing these leaders with others more willing to serve under American tutelage and more willing to prosecute the war against the NLF. At a press conference on 17 July 1963, Kennedy stated his preferred course clearly: 'We are not going to withdraw from [this] effort. In my opinion, for us to withdraw would mean a collapse not only of South Vietnam, but of Southeast Asia. So we are going to stay there' [144 *II p. 824*].

## NO NHUS IS GOOD NEWS

Unfortunately for Kennedy, the situation in South Vietnam continued to deteriorate as the summer wore on. By August, the war had become a critical policy problem for the White House. The Diem government's authority in large parts of the countryside had largely disappeared, and near-chaos gripped many cities. Dissident South Vietnamese army officers began plotting a coup, and their plans received a boost after the brutal and highly unpopular government raids on Buddhist pagodas in Hué, Saigon, and other cities on 21 August. American officials saw the raids as proof of Nhu's increasing authority in the Saigon government, and a number, including the assistant secretary of state for far eastern affairs, Roger Hilsman (he had succeeded Harriman earlier in the year), and the new American ambassador to South Vietnam, Henry Cabot Lodge, now argued that at least Nhu had to go [*Doc. 13*]. With Kennedy's authorization, the State Department informed Lodge that he should work to persuade Diem of the necessity of removing Nhu (and, in the process, the embarrassing Madame Nhu); if he did not, the cable observed, 'we must face the possibility that Diem himself cannot be preserved.' Diem refused to act, and by the final days of August, JFK had authorized the dissident generals to proceed with the coup.

No coup occurred. Not then. The generals harbored suspicions of one another's loyalties, and concerns about the level of American support. But in the three months that followed – a period culminating in Kennedy's death in Dallas on 22 November – US relations with the Saigon regime continued to deteriorate and coup planning revived, both in Washington and Saigon. It is in these three months that some authors say Kennedy made a secret decision to get out of Vietnam in the short term, regardless of the state of the war. A close examination of the documentary evidence for these three months, however, reveals little sign of an actual *intention* to withdraw. Two themes stand out in these months, which together are a powerful argument for a steadfast Kennedy still committed to staying in Vietnam.

The first theme is the palpable fear among senior American officials, including Kennedy, of premature negotiations for an end to the war. When Charles de Gaulle issued his public call for such a solution in late August, US officials, far from being enticed and/or relieved, were acutely alarmed. Mindful of de Gaulle's important place on the international stage, and of France's continuing cultural and social influence in Vietnam, these men worried that de Gaulle's comments, coming as they did at a time of growing chaos in the South, would find support in the world community and in Vietnam itself. Throughout the fall, representatives of the administration strove unsuccessfully to convince the French president to alter his stance or at least keep quiet about it. When the influential American columnist Walter Lippmann voiced support for de Gaulle's desire to move the struggle from the military to the political sphere, as had been done in Laos, senior officials expressed displeasure. And when the *New York Times* began advocating neutralization for Vietnam in its editorials, administration spokesmen were sent to the paper to convey White House opposition [*Doc. 14*].

This American trepidation about premature negotiations – premature because the Saigon government could not possibly enter talks in an advantageous position, given the political instability in the South and the increasing NLF strength – grew stronger when the CIA reported new rumors that Ngo Dinh Nhu was having secret contacts with the NLF and Hanoi for a possible accommodation. The meaning and importance of these contacts remains a matter of dispute, but there can be no doubting the acute fear with which American officials greeted them. Far from seeing possibilities in de Gaulle's proposal, they refused even to consider resolving the conflict at the conference table. An administration genuinely interested in negotiations might have imaginatively exploited the very vagueness of the French leader's pronouncement; a president determined to withdraw from South Vietnam would at least have given the plan serious thought. Most telling of all, when Ngo Dinh Nhu began exploring a settlement on his own, the administration, far from being encouraged, was deeply worried. Nhu's actions only made Washington more determined to overthrow him and his brother.

This brings us to the second theme of this August–November 1963 period: Kennedy's quiet but firm endorsement and encouragement of a showdown between Diem and dissident generals, which culminated in a *coup d'état* against Diem and Nhu on 1 November and their murder the next day. In September and October, Kennedy appears to have more or less resigned himself to the necessity of removing the regime. When on occasion he expressed uncertainty about a coup, it was primarily because of a fear that it might fail. An important question here is whether JFK understood that American complicity in a coup would increase US responsibility for subsequent developments in South Vietnam, thereby making withdrawal more difficult. The answer remains elusive, in part because neither he nor his advisers appear to have given the issue much thought. Before Diem's ouster, Kennedy seems to have believed that a change in government could actually *hasten* an American withdrawal – the new leaders would implement needed reforms, win increased popular support at the expense of the Vietcong, and allow the United States to reduce and eventually eliminate its presence in the South. After the coup he may have continued in this belief, but he also felt that this scenario would, even in the best of circumstances, take many months to materialize. In the short term, Kennedy understood, the US commitment was deeper than ever before, especially in view of the Ngos' murder. In a cable to Lodge on 6 November, JFK acknowledged American complicity in the coup and spoke of US 'responsibility' to help the new government succeed.

The connection between these two dominant themes is close. The fear of early negotiations – in particular, the fear that Diem and Nhu might be abandoning the war effort altogether, in favor of a negotiated settlement – contributed significantly to the decision to encourage the coup plotters.

The great preponderance of the evidence, then, would appear to refute any notion that Kennedy had decided firmly to withdraw from the conflict in Vietnam, win or lose, at the time he was gunned down. If one sought still more such evidence one might point to the administration's repeated public affirmations in the fall of 1963 of the importance of South Vietnam to US security and of the administration's determination to stand firm. Time and again in these months senior officials struck a firm tone in their public pronouncements. Oliver Stone's motion picture *JFK* shows a clip of Kennedy telling newsman Walter Cronkite on 9 September that, 'In the final analysis, it is their [the South Vietnamese] war. They are the ones that are going to have to win it or lose it.' Roger Hilsman and others have also pointed to this statement as proof of the president's intention to get out of the war. However, the preparatory memoranda for the Cronkite interview leave no doubt that the administration hoped to use it primarily to put pressure on the Diem regime, to bring Saigon officials into line by making them fear a drastic reduction in American assistance, a reduction never seriously contemplated.

Moreover, in the *very same interview* Kennedy also stated that it would be a mistake for the United States to withdraw. In subsequent weeks he continued publicly to vow steadfastness and to oppose withdrawal. His remarks set for delivery on 22 November at the Dallas Trade Mart, a destination he never reached, included the words: 'We in this country in this generation are the watchmen on the walls of freedom ... . Our assistance to ... nations can be painful, risky and costly, as is true in Southeast Asia today. But we dare not weary of the task.' The point here is not to deny assertions by Kennedy sympathizers that public comments may tell us very little about private planning and intentions; it is, rather, to suggest that the constant public affirmations by Kennedy and his associates of the Vietnam struggle's importance to US security served to reduce further their room for maneuver. And a Kennedy committed to disengaging from the conflict would surely want as much maneuverability as possible [123].

Most likely, John F. Kennedy on the day of his death had reached no final decision on what to do with his Vietnam problem. Like many politicians, he liked to postpone difficult decisions for as long as possible (prudence calls, in the bureaucratic phrase, for 'keeping options open'), and in late 1963 he could still temporize, could still hope that the Indochina crisis would somehow resolve itself, if not before the 1964 election, then after. America's presence in the war had expanded dramatically on his watch, but his decisions had usually been compromise decisions, between two extremes he seemed to fear in equal measure: an Americanized war or an American withdrawal. The following year, his brother Robert would be asked to describe how the administration would have responded to the prospect of a complete deterioration in South Vietnam. 'We'd cross that bridge when we came to it,' he replied. It is a phrase that effectively captures John F. Kennedy's whole approach to the war.

# CHAPTER FIVE

# THE COMING OF MAJOR WAR

Lyndon Johnson knew from the start of his administration that Vietnam was going to be one of his major foreign policy concerns. Since visiting Saigon as Kennedy's vice-president in the late spring of 1961, he had followed the course of the war and the evolution of American policy, and had sat in on many White House meetings. As he began his presidency he understood well the scope of America's commitment in Vietnam, and the potential trouble the war could pose for him. In a 2 December memorandum to Maxwell Taylor, the chairman of the JCS, LBJ noted that the more he looked at it, 'the more it is clear to me that South Vietnam is our most critical military area right now' [205 IV p. 651]. Three days later, in a brief speech at the State Department, Johnson exhorted his listeners to 'let no day go by without asking whether we are doing everything we can to win the struggle there.'

Johnson had been against the overthrow of Ngo Dinh Diem, but he was determined to carry out his predecessor's policies, particularly in the foreign arena and particularly in the difficult early months of transition. More important, he came to the White House with a deep and unquestioning commitment to the posture of staunch anti-communism, as well as to presidential supremacy in foreign policy. Though not ignorant of world affairs – as senator he had served on the Armed Services Committee – LBJ was uncomfortable with the intricacies of diplomacy and statecraft. He had gained valuable experience on foreign trips he took as vice-president, but very often these excursions only reinforced his insecurity about international politics. 'Foreigners,' Johnson quipped early in his administration, only half-jokingly, 'are not like the folks I am used to' [40; 89].

On Vietnam Johnson was from the start in 1954 a strong supporter of the attempt to create an anti-communist bastion in the southern half of the country. In 1961 he returned from Saigon militant on the need to persevere in the conflict and warning darkly that failure to act decisively could force the United States to retreat to San Francisco and 'leave the vast Pacific ... a Red Sea' [151]. He still adhered to that basic view when he assumed the presidency. Like many of his generation, Johnson was haunted by the failure of the allies to stop Hitler at Munich and he often declared he would not reward 'aggression' in Vietnam with 'appeasement.' He also invoked the mythology of the Alamo, where, as he said, Texas boys had 'fought for freedom.'

Shortly after becoming president, Johnson discussed the stakes in Vietnam with a young aide, Bill Moyers. The Chinese and Soviets would be watching the new administration, LBJ said. 'They'll be taking the measure of us. They'll be wondering just how far they can go.' What are you going to do?' Moyers asked. 'I'm going to give those fellas out there [in South Vietnam] the money they want,' Johnson replied. 'I told them I'm not going to let Vietnam go the way of China. I told them to go back and tell those generals in Saigon that Lyndon Johnson intends to stay by our word. But, by God, I want them to get off their butts and get out in those jungles and whip hell out of some Communists' [119 *p. 269*].

What is more, Johnson's political experience taught him the importance of taking a strong anti-communist stand in foreign policy if he were to have any hope of enacting social legislation at home – the Civil Rights Act, Medicare, the anti-poverty program, pending bills that could transform America. His oft-cited comment to biographer Doris Kearns was of dubious historical accuracy, but it conveys the point: 'I knew that Harry Truman and Dean Acheson had lost their effectiveness from the day that the communists took over in China. I believed that the loss of China had played a large role in the rise of Joe McCarthy. And I knew that all these problems, taken together, were chickenshit compared to what might happen if we lost Vietnam' [110 *pp. 252–3*].

Johnson retained Kennedy's top Vietnam advisers, and all of them urged staying the course in Vietnam. But the man who set the tone for Vietnam policy in those early days was Johnson himself. 'Win the war,' was the message he sent to his aides. It was a message he would continue to sound in the fateful months that followed. Yet Johnson also insisted that victory had to come quietly – that is, without a major escalation of the American commitment. As much as possible, he wanted Vietnam to be kept on the back-burner in those early months. There was to be a presidential election in 1964, and LBJ focused from the first on maximizing his chances to score big in November. This meant no new departures in foreign policy if at all possible and playing to his strength, domestic policy.

For the next twelve months, the Johnson team would struggle to reconcile these twin directives: to turn the war around while keeping it from becoming Americanized. They realized early that the two could not be reconciled, at which point the objective shifted to avoiding major escalation until after the November election. This goal they would meet, though just barely [121].

A BLEAK PICTURE

Johnson learned right away how severe was the disintegration in South Vietnam. On the battlefield, the situation was grim. The new president had barely settled into the Oval Office before the CIA, the Joint Chiefs of Staff, and the embassy in Saigon began issuing reports of virtually unchecked momentum by the Vietcong in many parts of South Vietnam. The picture was especially bleak in several key provinces around Saigon. 'The only progress made in Long An Province during the month of November 1963,' Lodge reported, 'has been by the Communist Viet Cong.' On 13 December, the Defense Intelligence Agency reported that the Vietcong had steadily raised their capabilities in 1963.

Troubling as these trends were to US officials in Washington and Saigon, even more disconcerting was the ambivalence of the new Saigon government led by Duong Van Minh with regard to the war effort, ambivalence which had first materialized in early November but which accelerated in December. Some American officials professed confidence that the present problems were the inevitable by-product of the transition to a new government, and that dramatic improvement would come soon. But a growing number ascribed the lack of progress to the regime's reluctance to initiate offensive military actions. Among the latter were General Harkins and the rest of the American military in Vietnam. Harkins had opposed the overthrow of the Ngos, and he made no secret of his dislike of Minh. He inundated administration officials in Washington with detailed information on the junta's non-aggressiveness; with time, many of those who had most opposed Diem and most welcomed the change in government would be converted to this view [17; 121].

The Minh regime's own actions contributed to this American perception by taking a number of steps to shift the struggle from the military to the political plane. Certain that the Diem regime's strategic hamlet program had done little except heighten the dissatisfaction in the countryside, for example, they announced plans for a rural-welfare program that would eventually supersede the hamlets, and they registered strong opposition when US military officials in Saigon floated a plan to improve the battlefield situation by bombing the North. Such bombing would not help win the war, Minh officials said, and would alienate popular opinion in the South.

Were members of the Minh junta interested in an early negotiated settlement with the NLF and Hanoi? Some of them were, but it does not appear that Minh himself was ready for such a move. As it had when Diem and Nhu appeared to consider the idea, however, the mere possibility of a political settlement struck fear into American officials. They worried when the CIA in the final weeks of 1963 found signs of RVN support for accommodation, and when the NLF issued its own conciliatory statements calling for negotiations to reach a cease-fire, free general elections, and the subsequent formation of a coalition government 'composed of representatives of all parties, tendencies, and strata of the South Vietnamese people' [21].

Equally disconcerting to the Johnson administration, influential voices within the United States were in the final weeks of the year coming to question the viability of continuing the US commitment to the war. Key senators, including Majority Leader Mike Mansfield (Democrat, Montana), Armed Services Committee chairman Richard Russell (Democrat, Georgia), and Foreign Relations Committee chairman J. William Fulbright (Democrat, Arkansas), told LBJ in December that he should seek a negotiated settlement. In the press, influential columnist Walter Lippmann and the editorial page of the *New York Times* urged the same thing. On 8 December the *Times* declared that 'a negotiated settlement and "neutralization" of Vietnam are not to be ruled out.'

But the administration did rule them out, as was made clear from its actions as the year turned. In December Johnson dispatched Robert McNamara on a fact-finding mission to South Vietnam, and the defense secretary came back warning of increased war weariness and support for neutralism among southerners but urging a steadfast US commitment to the war [Doc. 15]. On 2 January, an interdepartmental committee recommended the implementation of OPLAN 34-A, which, by 'progressively escalating pressure ... to inflict increasing punishment upon North Vietnam,' might convince Hanoi 'to desist from its aggressive policies.' The plan was to be directed by the military and was to consist of three phases over the next calendar year, each phase progressively more punitive. Top administration officials doubted that the measures would cause Hanoi to cease its support for the Vietcong, but they counseled Johnson to approve the plan nonetheless. He obliged, signing off on the scheme on 16 January [134].

## REASSESSMENT IN HANOI – AND IN ALLIED CAPITALS

That Johnson was as determined as his predecessor to win the war in Vietnam was not lost on the leadership in Hanoi. Ho Chi Minh and his colleagues had possessed great hopes after the ouster of the Diem regime and the death of Kennedy. Perhaps, they hoped, the succeeding weeks would witness a spontaneous uprising in the South in support of reconciliation with the North, or perhaps an American withdrawal ordered by the new US president, or both.

Neither happened, and at the Ninth Plenum of the Vietnamese Workers' Party in December 1963 northern leaders analyzed the situation and debated where to go from here. The debate was lively, and probably acrimonious. Some members apparently advocated the introduction of North Vietnamese main force troops into the South to help bring the Saigon regime to its knees, while others were reluctant to do anything that might strain relations with Hanoi's chief allies, China and the Soviet Union, and which might increase risk of major US intervention. In the end, the Central Committee approved a plan that called for the rapid strengthening of the Vietcong in the hope of achieving a decisive shift in the balance of forces and realizing victory in a short period of time.

Hanoi leaders made these decisions not because they saw a military confrontation involving large-scale units as inevitable, but because they hoped a forceful response would prevent such a confrontation from occurring. They still sought to avoid a major escalation of the war resulting in the entry of American ground forces. Accordingly, they continued in late 1963 and into 1964 to look favorably upon a negotiated settlement that would allow a US disengagement from South Vietnam. Resolution 9 of the meeting spoke of the possibility that the revolution might have to go through a lengthy period of 'complex forms and methods' of struggle before victory was attained, which one discerning historian has called 'an obvious allusion to the possibility of a negotiated settlement.' Final victory would be reached via an incremental 'step-by-step' process, a 'transition period' of uncertain length [53].

Western allied leaders too perceived the new American administration's determination on the war, and it worried them. Sympathetic in some instances to Washington's broad aims in the conflict, most governments nevertheless doubted that the aims could be achieved at any kind of reasonable cost – and indeed that it was necessary even to try. As a result, 1964 would witness a steady diminution of world support for US policy in Vietnam, to the point that by autumn America would be essentially isolated in the international community.

Why the decline in support during that pivotal year? In large measure because of developments within South Vietnam. The year would mark the low point in the ten-year history of South Vietnam, in which the RVN's fortunes and the ARVN's will to fight diminished dramatically. War weariness and attachment to 'neutralism' (meaning, in this context, a swift end to the war on whatever terms) among the peasantry and many urbanites became rampant. Already in January and February, one finds evidence that Washington decision-makers were more committed to the war than were the mass of the South Vietnamese they were ostensibly there to help; by the end of the year, that evidence would be stronger still. Even Nguyen Khanh, who assumed the leadership in Saigon after a bloodless *coup d'état* at the end of January, would in time fall out of favor with the Americans for failing in their eyes to be vigorous enough in prosecuting the war. Like the Diem regime and the Minh junta before him, Khanh would learn that his ability to win broad-based domestic support would be directly linked to his ability to preserve a degree of independence from the United States.

Changes outside South Vietnam also influenced allied thinking about Indochina and what ought to happen there. The Sino-Soviet split had grown wider and deeper in 1963, and in the minds of many observers this development opened up opportunities for facilitating a political solution to the conflict in Vietnam. The reduced tensions in the Soviet–American relationship also suggested to some, including the United Nations (UN) secretary-general, U Thant, that conflicts in Third World nations need no longer loom as important in superpower politics as they once did. Hence the equanimity with which most Western leaders reacted to the French government's decision to extend recognition in January 1964 to the People's Republic of China. While Washington officials tried to dissuade Paris from following through with the plan, Canadian and British officials quietly assured the French that they had no objection to the move – the Canadian prime minister, Lester Pearson, indeed told Charles de Gaulle that he hoped Ottawa too could extend recognition to Beijing soon [121].

France's continued opposition to American policy in Southeast Asia was a source of concern to US officials – particularly in view of the considerable cultural and social influence that the French retained in Vietnam – but they were more worried about the prospect of a break with Britain over the war. In the early months of 1964, the London government's trepidations increased, particularly as it learned that Washington was giving serious consideration to taking the war to North Vietnam in an effort to turn the tide. British officials from top to bottom believed such action would have little impact on the insurgency in the South, and would cause China and the Soviet Union to increase their assistance to Hanoi. A study by the British Joint Intelligence Committee in late February concluded that even a complete severance of all links between North Vietnam and the Vietcong in the South (which the report called virtually impossible to bring about) would not significantly reduce the problem of defeating the insurgents, given their basic self-sufficiency. Moreover, an attack on the North would strengthen Hanoi–Beijing relations, would bring increased Chinese and Soviet assistance to the DRV, and would generate widespread condemnation in the international community [121].

Moreover, it annoyed the British that the Americans had done little or nothing to prevent the coup that overthrew the Minh junta – in London's view, Minh was far superior to Khanh as a leader, and two coups in such quick succession meant that much more governmental disruption, that much more chaos at the regional and local administrative levels. Though the London government was no more prepared than in 1963 to challenge Washington overtly over Vietnam – the risks were too great, especially given America's crucial role in propping up the beleaguered pound – neither could the Johnson administration count on more than tepid rhetorical support for its policy. Almost certainly, London's clear opposition to bombing the North played an important part in Johnson's decision in early March to postpone any such action for the future.

SEEKING 'MORE FLAGS'

With an early expansion of the war off the table, Washington officials looked for other ways to bolster the Saigon government and demonstrate determination to leaders in Hanoi. One way they did so was through the 'More Flags' campaign, an effort launched by the State Department in April 1964 designed to get increased allied contributions to the war effort.

The campaign was a failure from the start. When Dean Rusk asked NATO members for at least token material and manpower participation in the conflict at an alliance meeting at The Hague in May 1964, he found a decidedly unenthusiastic response. Some members agreed to provide very modest amounts of non-military support to the South Vietnamese regime, but all refused to send any troops. In the wake of the meeting, Rusk ordered embassy staff in key capitals to press the host governments for greater participation in the struggle. The cable to the Bonn embassy, for example, instructed staffers to inform West German officials that their country's contribution to the war effort was insufficient; that a German embassy in Saigon needed to be constructed immediately and 'with suitable publicity and fanfare'; and that Bonn needed to make a 'public commitment of additional aid to GVN [South Vietnam].' The Germans ruled out a major aid package and were non-committal even about a small one. In London, officials likewise resisted strong American pressure for a stepped-up British commitment [121].

Canada, too, registered concerns about the direction of American policy. When US and Canadian officials met in Ottawa in late May to go over the message that Canadian diplomat J. Blair Seaborn would convey to the North Vietnamese during a visit to Hanoi a few weeks later, the external affairs minister, Paul Martin, expressed trepidation. Canadians would not look kindly on the prospect of an enlarged war, Martin told the State Department's William Sullivan, and he insisted that Seaborn should not have to 'agree with or associate his Government with the substance of some of the messages' he would be transmitting, so long as he transmitted them faithfully. Martin further said he agreed with American columnist Walter Lippmann's most recent column, in which Lippmann said that even an imperfect political settlement via a conference was preferable to pursuing a costly and unwinnable war. How could Lyndon Johnson avoid a confer-ence, Martin asked Sullivan, particularly when the only alternative seemed to be direct military intervention? Sullivan's response was telling. These were 'extreme alternatives,' he said, and the administration hoped to find a middle way. But he acknowledged that intervention seemed a more likely course than a conference at the present time. Martin was unmoved. He repeated Canadian objections to direct intervention and repeated his view that a conference, perhaps including the whole of Indochina, seemed the best bet [121].

To be sure, this unwillingness of allied governments to become meaningfully involved in supporting the Saigon government was not quite universal. Australia boosted its financial and manpower commitment significantly in early June and urged Washington in the strongest terms to continue steadfast in the war. But the Australians were unique. Other governments declined altogether to provide assistance, or made vague pledges of limited future support, almost invariably of a token character and in the end often not kept. Washington analysts understood only too well that these attitudes represented further proof of fundamental international doubts about the importance of Indochina to the West's security, as well as concerns about the dangers of an escalated war, and that any US expansion of the war was therefore a perilous proposition.

Even in Asia, Washington could not count on strong support. Japan was pessimistic about the RVN's prospects and opposed to an escalated war, as was Pakistan, a member of SEATO. Burma and India favored negotiations leading to neutralization, either for South Vietnam alone or for a reunified Vietnam, while in Cambodia, Prince Sihanouk had since late 1963 called for neutralization for his country and for the rest of Indochina as well.

TONKIN GULF

The problems in the 'More Flags' campaign in the summer of 1964 reinforced the Johnson administration's desire to postpone any major escalation of the war. But it was not the chief factor in that decision – more important was Lyndon Johnson's strong desire to avoid drastic measures in Vietnam (in whatever direction) prior to the fall election, as well as serious American concerns that the Khanh government in Saigon was too weak to sustain a wider war. Khanh had struggled since taking power at the end of January to gain legitimacy for his government and to bring cohesion and motivation to the ARVN. In June and July he began pressing the United States for an expansion of the war to the North; the Americans, led by the new ambassador in Saigon, General Maxwell Taylor, deflected these entreaties. They did so not because they had changed their minds about the likely necessity of expanding the war. On the contrary, a consensus existed among senior policy-makers that wider military action would at some point be necessary. But the time had not yet come.

By late July, Khanh was desperate. He began warning that he might abandon the premiership if he could not get Washington to go along with an attack on the North. Other observers, too, saw events at the end of July moving to a climax, of one kind or another. Several pointed to a *Saigon Daily News* article of 26 July which said that, without an attack on the North, neutralism would triumph. 'Who can blame [the people], then, if they succumb to the temptations of de Gaulle's promises?' the paper asked. On 30 July, the *News* said the South Vietnamese people were tired of dying in an apparently hopeless cause. Canadian and British officials in Saigon speculated in late July that Khanh now realized he lacked the prestige and experience to lead his people through a long war and therefore sought a radical solution: either an attack on the DRV or a negotiated deal with the NLF [121].

Something had to happen, all observers could agree. Within days, something did. In the first days of August 1964, a crisis in the Gulf of Tonkin off the coast of North Vietnam brought the first direct use of American naval and air power against North Vietnam. On the 2nd and the 4th of that month, two US destroyers in the Gulf reported attacks by North Vietnamese patrol boats. The first attack – on the *Maddox* – came hard on the heels of a South Vietnamese raid on DRV territory, itself part of the American OPLAN 34-A program aimed at pressuring Hanoi to cease its support of the insurgency. Most likely, North Vietnamese officials assumed that the US navy was participating in the raid. Three torpedoes were fired on the *Maddox*, but none found its target. In response, the *Maddox* opened fire, damaging two patrol boats and sinking a third [134].

When word of the incident reached the White House, President Johnson sent a stern warning to Hanoi warning of 'grave consequences' should additional 'unprovoked' attacks occur. He also ordered a second destroyer, the *C. Turner Joy*, to join the *Maddox* in the patrol in the Gulf. Two nights later, on 4 August, the commander of the *C. Turner Joy* believed that his destroyer was under fire and ordered his gunners to return fire. They did so but hit nothing, almost certainly because no attack in fact had occurred. The commander of the *Maddox* urged that the event be thoroughly reviewed before any decision be made on reprisal action.

Johnson would have none of it. With considerably less than the full facts in front of him, the president ordered air strikes against selected North Vietnamese patrol boat bases and an oil depot, and declared in a televised speech: 'Aggression unchallenged is aggression unleashed.' The air attack, described as 'limited in scale,' was made up of 64 sorties which destroyed or damaged 25 patrol boats. In addition, Johnson ordered aides to rework and prepare to introduce a long-existing congressional authorization on the use of force. On 7 August, after little debate, Congress gave the president broad authority 'to take all necessary measures' and 'all necessary steps' to defend US forces in Southeast Asia and stop aggression. Only two law-makers voted no: Senators Wayne Morse of Oregon and Ernest Gruening of Alaska, both Democrats [*Doc. 16*].

Johnson was delighted with the broad authority the resolution gave him. 'Like grandma's nightshirt,' he later quipped, 'it covered everything.' Even more pleasing, the public evidently shared Congress's approval – over-night his ratings in a Louis Harris public opinion poll shot up 30 percent. For the general public, confused about what was happening in South Vietnam, the North Vietnamese attack and massive US retaliation must have seemed satisfyingly clear. Of course, like members of Congress, the people had not been told the whole story – they did not know of the OPLAN 34-A covert operations then under way against North Vietnam, or of the plans being laid for escalation. Few understood the implications of the administration's actions. And that was just the way the president and his men preferred it. In their view they could scarcely have scripted the affair any better, for Johnson now possessed not only unsurpassed authority to wage war in a remote region far from America's shores, but his popu-larity had skyrocketed as well. 'I didn't just screw Ho Chi Minh, I cut his pecker off,' Johnson whispered to a reporter the day after the air strikes [81 *p. 414*].

Well, no. The North Vietnamese were indeed alarmed by the flexing of American muscle in the Gulf, and believed it represented the first stage in a major US escalation. They responded, however, by increasing significantly their commitment of men and resources to the struggle in the South. The first People's Army of Vietnam (PAVN) regiment started down the Ho Chi Minh Trail in September, and the second followed a month later. Hanoi also undertook to upgrade the Trail to allow men and matériel to move more easily to the South, and to beef up anti-aircraft defenses in North Vietnam. The Chinese meanwhile responded to the incident by, among other things, initiating a major expansion of the railroad network north of the Vietnamese border; as a result, the North Vietnamese would henceforth have a much easier time obtaining needed supplies should the port of Haiphong become unusable. All in all, historian Edwin E. Moïse has perceptively argued, by the time the Johnson administration actually imple-mented its major escalation of US involvement in February and March 1965, enemy forces 'were stronger, better prepared, and better supplied than they would have been had the Tonkin Gulf incidents never occurred' [134 *p. 253*].

Nor did the retaliatory bombing have the desired impact on South Vietnamese attitudes. The hope had been that the strong US response would bolster Nguyen Khanh's government and boost the morale among the populace in the South, but nothing of the kind happened. In the last half of August and September, American officials in Saigon and Washington continued to fret about Khanh's lack of popular support and the evidence of growing war weariness in both the urban and rural areas of South Vietnam. For a time in late August, it appeared that the RVN might simply cease to exist: Khanh resigned, then apparently suffered a mental and physical 'breakdown' a few days later, then gave in to American pressure and agreed to resume power. Meanwhile, long-simmering hatreds and suspicions between Catholics and Buddhists flared into street fighting in several cities, and students took to the streets in ever larger numbers, throwing bottles and rocks and shouting 'Down with Nhuyen Khanh.' On the military battlefield, the Vietcong scored several easy victories against dispirited ARVN forces.

The White House could at least take solace from one thing: the forceful American response in the Gulf effectively removed Vietnam as a campaign issue in the presidential race that autumn. Republican front-runner Barry Goldwater had spend the summer months advocating a stronger show of American force in the war; now that Johnson had delivered, if only briefly, Goldwater had difficulty making the war an issue. In the weeks leading up to the vote, Johnson pledged to continue to support South Vietnam in its struggle but also vowed that American boys should not be sent to fight Asian wars. It was a reassuring message, and it helped Johnson to a landslide win – he won 44 states and 61 percent of the vote, and his plurality was the largest in American history. The Democratic Party added two seats in the Senate, making a total of 68 (against 32 for the Republicans), and gained 37 in the House of Representatives, giving it 297 (against the Republicans' 140).

## CHOICE AND DECISION

What would the landslide mean for America's Vietnam policy? That was the question of the moment, as observers all over the world understood. All year long, analysts in the key world capitals – London, Paris, Moscow, Ottawa, Beijing, Hanoi – had subscribed to the view that Lyndon Johnson would try hard to avoid dramatic policy moves on Vietnam before the election. After voting day, however, tough decisions would have to be made. Particularly as the war effort in South Vietnam deteriorated in the summer and early fall of 1964, and the political in-fighting in Saigon and general war weariness among southerners increased, analysts both inside and outside the United States saw a fundamental choice facing whoever might be the victorious candidate: whether to expand dramatically the American involvement in the conflict or to seek some kind of face-saving exit from South Vietnam. Judgments about the moral or geostrategic correctness of US policy mattered little here: supporters as well as critics of America's commitment to the Saigon government agreed these were the likely alternatives.

Which way would the president go? To the international diplomatic community and to many close observers in the United States, who did not know the details of the administration's secret planning, it was very much an open question. An expanded war was in no way preordained. Escalation versus disengagement constituted an odious choice but also a legitimate one, which meant US officials had considerable freedom of maneuver about which way to go. Had these analysts been able to predict the size of Johnson's victory they would no doubt have been further convinced of this fundamental maneuverability.

Inside the upper reaches of the administration, however, there was little sense of that maneuverability. Johnson did order the convening of an NSC interagency 'Working Group' (chaired by the assistant secretary of state for far eastern affairs, William P. Bundy) whose task it would be to explore American options on Vietnam, but he also made clear that he was no less determined than before to prevail in the war. Presidential aides understood this Johnsonian determination perfectly well, and it must have exerted a powerful influence over the Working Group's deliberation. In addition, almost all of these advisers had themselves developed a deep stake in the success of the war effort. For several years in many cases, they had trumpeted the need to stand firm and proclaimed the certainty of ultimate victory, and to suggest a new course now would mean going against all their previous recommendations and analyses.

As a result, the defining characteristic of the post-election deliberations was their highly circumscribed nature. Whatever freedom of action other observers may have thought Johnson possessed after the crushing victory over Goldwater, it quickly became clear that there remained little latitude for reopening the basic questions about American involvement in Vietnam, about whether the struggle needed to be won or whether it could be won. The range of options under consideration was narrow – all of them presupposed the need to stand firm.

Even as they continued to embrace old assumptions about Vietnam's importance and the need to persevere, however, senior American planners also understood that the war had entered a new stage, requiring new measures. In the fall months of 1964, the politico-military situation in South Vietnam had continued to deteriorate. There were frequent changes at the top levels of the Saigon government, and the ARVN continued to be racked by dissension among officers and low morale and high desertion rates among troops. War weariness was widespread in both urban areas and among the peasantry, and diplomats and reporters in Saigon noted a sharp rise in anti-American sentiment. Meanwhile, the Vietcong scored more and more gains, with the result that by the end of the year many important roads in the Mekong Delta, some only a few miles from Saigon, were now more or less permanently cut off by Vietcong roadblocks or trenches dug across the right of way. Long An province, directly south of Saigon, which had received the highest priority for American assistance of any province in South Vietnam during 1964, was now much less secure than it had been at the time of Diem's overthrow a year earlier. In the northern provinces, which a year earlier had been considered largely secure, the situation had deteriorated severely.

Hence the outcome of the post-election deliberations in Washington: a decision to implement a two-phase escalatory policy aimed at turning the war around. The first phase would involve 'armed reconnaissance strikes' against infiltration routes in Laos as well as retaliatory strikes against the North in the event of a Vietcong 'spectacular,' while the second would see 'graduated military pressure' against North Vietnam. Phase One would begin as soon as possible. Phase Two would come later, some time after thirty days, provided the Saigon government had bettered its effectiveness 'to an acceptable degree.' Unwilling to contemplate the implications if the regime should fail to meet this standard, however, the advisory team then proceeded to waive this requirement: 'If the GVN [RVN] can only be kept going by stronger action,' the final recommendations read, then 'the U.S. is prepared ... to enter into a second phase program.' Escalation, in other words, should be undertaken regardless of the political picture in Saigon, either to reward the Saigon regime or to keep it from disintegrating [209].

Would US ground forces be part of this second phase of the escalation? In the minds of most officials, yes. To a degree not appreciated in most historical accounts, key players anticipated from the start of these post-election deliberations that ground troops would be part of the equation. The position paper that emerged out of the crucial White House meeting on 1 December included the cryptic but suggestive line that the escalatory program would include 'appropriate U.S. deployments to handle any contingency.' A few days later, William Bundy told Australian and New Zealand officials that the adoption of Phase Two could lead to the stationing of one division or two battalions of US ground forces in the northern part of South Vietnam, to be based in and supplied from Danang. And late that month, Lyndon Johnson told his Saigon ambassador, Maxwell Taylor, that airpower alone could never win the war and that he was prepared to increase substantially the number of Americans fighting in Vietnam [*Doc. 17*] [121].

If a desire to give the RVN yet one more chance to get its act together was one rationale for a two-phase escalation, there was also another: a need to solidify support for US policy among the American people and key international audiences prior to any major expansion of the fighting. This too would be a tall task, senior planners knew. In the final weeks of 1964, domestic dissatisfaction with the Vietnam situation grew dramatically.

Scores of newspapers, some of which had hitherto been unquestioning supporters of the American commitment (and would be again after the Americanization of the war in 1965), began to express deep doubts about the enterprise. Many of them endorsed a negotiated disengagement from the war. Others would not go that far but still explicitly ruled out any deeper American involvement. A haunting question began to echo in editorials across the land: just what was America doing supporting a government and a people so demonstrably unwilling to contribute to their own defense?

On Capitol Hill, meanwhile, support increased for a full-fledged re-examination of the country's commitment to South Vietnam, especially among Johnson's own Democrats. The party's foreign policy leaders in the Senate, including Richard Russell, Mike Mansfield, J. William Fulbright, and Frank Church, each cautioned the administration in December against deepening US involvement in the conflict and urged that all avenues for disengagement be sought. In the Senate as a whole, confusion reigned. An Associated Press poll of 83 Senators found no consensus whatsoever on what the Vietnam problem was or what the United States ought to do about it. Three of the respondents fully supported expansion of the war into North Vietnam, while five suggested American troops could be sent to the South at some future date if the situation warranted it. Ten advocated an immediate move to negotiations. Three wanted a unilateral American withdrawal. Eight senators said they simply did not know what to do. Others refused to comment for the present, many on the grounds that they wanted to wait for the results of inquiries by the Senate.

Nor did the administration find success with its intensified effort to get international support for the South Vietnamese cause. As part of the two-phase policy Johnson ordered the 'More Flags' campaign stepped up, but the results were as meager as ever. Most friendly governments continued to offer tepid rhetorical support for America's mission in Vietnam but rule out meaningful assistance to the cause. When the new British prime minister, Harold Wilson, visited Washington in December 1964, he affirmed Britain's support for current US policy but warned against any expansion of the war and resisted strong pressure from Johnson to commit manpower to the struggle. In advance of Japanese leader Eisaku Sato's visit the following month, a NSC memo warned that even in conservative circles in Japan 'there are serious misgivings about the prospects for success of U.S. Southeast Asia policies and the long-term risk to Japan in over-commitment to the U.S. position.' During his talks with American officials, Sato pledged support for current levels of US assistance to South Vietnam but voiced opposition to American bombing attacks on the DRV, on the grounds that such attacks would fail to achieve their objectives and would send the wrong message to the peoples of Asia. The same basic sentiments were voiced privately by the Canadian government in December 1964 and January 1965 [121].

In Paris, Charles de Gaulle continued to press the argument that the sooner Washington agreed to negotiate, the better. When Secretary of State Dean Rusk called on him in Paris in mid-December 1964, the two men disagreed sharply on Vietnam, with Rusk insisting that communists could not be trusted and could never be neutral, and de Gaulle countering that neutrality was working, albeit imperfectly in Laos and Cambodia, and that no one could be sure it would not work in Vietnam. The Frenchman said Washington faced a key choice, whether to expand its involvement dramatically and thereby commit itself to a long and bloody – and ultimately unwinnable – war, or seek a negotiated way out. The United States should learn from the French experiences in Indochina and Algeria and 'eliminate this area from the Cold War,' he declared. Rusk replied that the fighting would end if Hanoi and Beijing just left their neighbors alone.

AN OPENING FOR DIPLOMACY?

Did these realities – the war weariness and anti-Americanism in South Vietnam, the domestic American frustration with the state of the war, and the growing American isolation on Vietnam among its allies – incline top administration officials to give negotiations a chance? No. That option was no more palatable to policy-makers than it had ever been. In September UN Secretary-General U Thant had won assurance from the DRV that it would enter talks but had been rebuffed by the United States. In November, with Johnson safely re-elected, Thant tried again, telling the American ambassador to the UN, Adlai Stevenson, that the Burmese government of Ne Win had agreed to serve as host for the talks. Stevenson was sympathetic and passed on the information to Secretary of State Dean Rusk. Now was not the time for talks with Hanoi, Rusk told him, and therefore the secretary-general should be told to put the idea on the shelf. Thant had been rejected again [160; 197].

Also in late November, the Canadian government asked Washington for a substantive message that J. Blair Seaborn could deliver to North Vietnamese officials during his upcoming visit to Hanoi. The administration showed little interest in the matter and gave Seaborn no real message to convey, beyond one affirming America's continued commitment to the RVN. Ottawa officials were dismayed. The Americans, they concluded, clearly preferred a military solution over a diplomatic one.

A large question here is whether the North Vietnamese were sincere in claiming to want a diplomatic settlement. It seems very likely that they were. As 1964 drew to a close, Ho Chi Minh and his colleagues remained steadfast in their determination to prevail in the conflict, and they were not keen on compromising their fundamental objectives in the struggle. Moreover, they saw little reason to compromise, given the growing chaos in the South. At the same time, the DRV leadership still sought to avert a large-scale American military intervention in the war, and they appear to have been prepared to compromise on non-fundamentals to achieve that objective – on the speed of the American withdrawal, for example, or the timing of reunification of the country.

Some weeks earlier, in October 1964, the prospect of a major escalation of the fighting was a subject of discussion when Pham Van Dong met Mao Zedong in Beijing. The two men agreed that Washington did not want to fight a major war. 'The United States is facing many difficulties, and it is not easy for it to expand the war,' Pham Van Dong said, no doubt referring both to the weak RVN base upon which such an escalation would be launched and the lack of enthusiasm for such a move among many in the United States and in Western capitals. 'We must adopt a very skillful strategy, and should not provoke [the US],' he said. This meant keeping the level of fighting at about its current level. 'If the United States dares to start a [larger] war, we will fight it,' Pham Van Dong assured Mao, 'and we will win it.' But it would be better if it did not come to that [213 *pp. 83–4*].

Mao agreed and said the more decisively a communist nation defeated a Western army, the more resigned the West felt to enter peace talks. 'For example,' he went on, 'you beat the French, and they became willing to negotiate with you.' The Algerians also beat France, and again the French agreed to talk. Even right now, Mao added, 'It is not completely a bad thing to negotiate. You have already earned the qualifications to negotiate. It is another matter whether or not the negotiation will succeed' [ibid.].

Therefore, in the aftermath of the American election Hanoi also sent subtle signals that it was open to peace talks. William Bundy acknowledged as much when he told Canadian officials in Washington on 3 December that Hanoi had been putting out hints in many quarters in November that it was interested in pursuing a settlement to the war, though only on its previously stated terms. Bundy did not indicate what those terms were, but likely he believed them to involve (1) a coalition government in Saigon, with prominent NLF representation; (2) American withdrawal; and (3) eventual reunification of the country under Hanoi's control. But within these terms there were gray areas, which could be the subject of discussion during bilateral talks or at a Geneva-type conference.

One year later, in the late autumn of 1965, U Thant's efforts in 1964 to facilitate negotiations became public knowledge. Senior US officials instantly knew they faced a sticky problem, and scrambled for a response. The disclosures, they realized, made them appear to have been not merely skeptical of a diplomatic settlement in Vietnam in late 1964, but actively opposed to such a solution. It made for a potentially serious public-relations issue.

People were certain to ask, Undersecretary of State George Ball said to a colleague, 'Why didn't you find out [what Hanoi had in mind]?' A satisfactory reply had to be found. Ball could not think of one [121].

The skeptical reader might interject here and say there was a perfectly satisfactory reply Ball might have given, one centering on the Soviet Union and China. In this line of analysis, the Vietnam War was never really about Vietnam at all but about the larger Cold War struggle between East and West. An American disengagement from Vietnam, so the argument goes, would have emboldened the leaders in Moscow and Beijing to act aggressively all over the globe. Hence the need to stand firm, even despite long odds and without allied support.

How did the Soviet Union and China view the conflict in Vietnam as 1964 turned into 1965, and how were their postures in turn viewed by the United States? For Moscow, Vietnam continued to present a pesky dilemma: how to affirm Soviet support for the North Vietnamese while preventing a large-scale expansion of the war. In October 1964, Nikita Khrushchev had been ousted as the USSR's leader in a Kremlin power struggle. The new leadership under Leonid Brezhnev and Alexei Kosygin sought to increase Soviet influence in the region (Soviet–North Vietnamese relations had plummeted in the first half of 1964, as Hanoi by and large took the Chinese side in the Sino-Soviet split), partly to counter growing Chinese influence and partly because they smelled a Communist victory in Vietnam and wanted to be able to claim part of the credit. At the same time, they feared a larger war that might force them to become more directly involved, or might bring the Chinese into the DRV in large numbers, and so they hoped to restrain both Washington and Hanoi from initiating a major escalation. On 9 December, Foreign Minister Andrei Gromyko told Rusk that America had no important stake in the Vietnam conflict and that none of the US-sponsored governments in Saigon had been worthy of the name. He told Rusk that all outstanding questions on the war could be solved at a great-power conference. Rusk responded with what was becoming his mantra on Vietnam: if Hanoi and Beijing would 'leave their neighbors alone,' peace would come [206 *I p. 502*].

Washington planners were well aware of the depth of the Sino-Soviet split and of Moscow's desire to discourage an expansion of the war in Vietnam. In the post-election policy deliberations both the split and the Soviet opposition to a wider war were taken as givens by most analysts. At the beginning of January 1965, William Bundy told Australian officials that in the US estimation the increased Russian interest in the war stemmed largely from the desire on the part of Kremlin leaders to redress the Sino/Soviet balance in Hanoi. Brezhnev and Kosygin wanted to keep the Chinese from expanding their influence in North Vietnam, Bundy said, and were sympathetic to any course – including negotiations – that would accomplish this aim.

With regard to China, its outlook and ambitions weighed on the minds of American officials in the closing weeks of 1964, but not as much as one might think – in the many hundreds of pages of memoranda produced in the Working Group policy discussions, it is startling how seldom analyses of China's posture and aims appear. When Beijing's intentions did come up for discussion, little consensus emerged. Some saw the Vietnam commitment as crucial in the effort to contain what they described as an expansionist China driven by internal need to expand. Others said Beijing's bark was worse than its bite, that its leaders were well aware of their country's military backwardness, and that Mao Zedong's main concern was keeping American power from encroaching on his southern frontier.

Tellingly, two key members of the Working Group appear to have had strong doubts that containing China required fighting a war in Vietnam. Near the end of the deliberations, top McNamara deputy John McNaughton and the State Department's William Bundy, while arguing against the option of merely continuing the present level of US involvement, conceded that this course might not bring disastrous results, especially given the deep Sino-Soviet split. Should the administration opt for the *status quo* and against the new military measures, the two men wrote, 'the most likely result would be a Vietnamese-negotiated deal, under which an eventually unified Communist Vietnam would reassert its traditional hostility to Communist China and limit its own ambitions to Laos and Cambodia.' An accurate description if ever there was one of post-1975 Vietnam, this assertion suggests that senior American officials were not convinced that checking Chinese power necessitated waging war in South Vietnam.

ESCALATION

At the start of 1965, then, several things were clear. One was that the mass of the South Vietnamese people were tired of twenty years of fighting and were anxious for an end to the war. Another was that the Saigon government was racked by internal division and its armed forces were characterized by high rates of desertion and a general unwillingness to engage the enemy. A third reality was that much of the international community favored an early negotiated settlement of the war but were unwilling to work hard to make it happen, while a fourth was that elite voices in the United States were unhappy about Vietnam and opposed to an enlarged American presence there. Finally, there was this: by the start of the year the Johnson administration had reached a broad – though still secret – decision to escalate dramatically US involvement in Vietnam, including, if necessary, deploying ground forces.

Of course, there is a difference between choosing a policy option and actually implementing that policy. And to suggest that Lyndon Johnson at the beginning of 1965 was prepared to escalate the Vietnam War, and was readying to do so, is not to suggest that he relished the idea, least of all then, at the start of his administration. He desperately hoped the Saigon political situation could be held together for at least a few weeks, so that he could delay having to implement the escalatory measures under Phase Two and instead focus his energies on moving forward with his ambitious domestic legislative agenda. What is more, he and his aides needed time to lay the necessary groundwork for escalation with Congress and the American people. In the first months of 1965, White House officials worked hard to convince skeptical lawmakers to support administration policy or at least keep their misgivings quiet, and to head off any move among Democratic leaders to hold a full-fledged Senate debate on the war.

They had better luck with this second task than with the first. Though many in Congress and the press called for a national debate on Vietnam in the first weeks of the year, none took place, in large part because of opposition from the administration. In South Vietnam, however, the RVN's political and military position deteriorated further despite Maxwell Taylor's efforts to get Saigon politicians to work together and bring some semblance of stability to the government. By late January, Johnson's top advisers were recommending the initiation of Phase Two. The president agreed. In early February he dispatched McGeorge Bundy to South Vietnam to get a first-hand account of the state of affairs, but the decision to expand the war had already been made [36].

Then came Pleiku. In Chapter 1 we asserted that the events surrounding Pleiku marked the cross-over point to an Americanized war in Vietnam. In the days thereafter, Washington moved to implement a policy of sustained aerial attacks on targets in North Vietnam and enemy-held areas in South Vietnam – Operation Rolling Thunder – and also sent the first American ground forces to the war. Hanoi and its chief allies, China and the Soviet Union, responded by becoming more hostile on the question of negotiations. As the bombing attacks increased in intensity and the number of American troops grew, the DRV responded by increasing the size and pace of its infiltration of men and matériel into the South. Escalation begat escalation.

Some had seen it coming. For a year or more, supporters as well as opponents of American involvement had warned that disengagement would be infinitely harder after the first ground forces were sent, for international as well as domestic American reasons. US credibility would be committed in a way it was not before. And indeed, in the spring of 1965, as the number of American casualties increased, Johnson faced greater partisan pressure than previously, as Republicans became more voluble in demanding victory. In those months he complained of feeling 'trapped' on Vietnam, with no place to go. He had said the same thing in 1964; this time it had more legitimacy.

The point should not be exaggerated. To say that Pleiku marked a threshold is not to say there was no turning back after that point. Decisions made can be unmade; thresholds crossed can be re-crossed. Vice-President Hubert H. Humphrey, distraught at the turn of events and filled with foreboding about the domestic political implications of a long and bloody war in Southeast Asia, wrote two prescient memos to Johnson in the weeks after Pleiku urging him to reduce rather than increase a commitment few Americans understood [*Doc. 18*]. Johnson was not interested in listening, even though Humphrey's line of argument was echoed by numerous other politicians – and influential elements in the American press – in these critical weeks. He was not interested in exploring his options, in probing the possibilities for an early political settlement. He told Humphrey, 'We don't need all these memos,' and proceeded to shut him out of Vietnam meetings for the better part of a year.

### THE JOHNS HOPKINS SPEECH

But if the president and his senior Vietnam advisers remained unwilling to undertake a fundamental re-evaluation of American policy in Vietnam, they understood that some kind of significant response needed to be made to the growing backlash against the escalation. In late March, in the wake of an anti-war teach-in at the University of Michigan and continued calls for a diplomatic solution from allied governments and from many in the press, Johnson's aides began drafting a major speech on American objectives in Vietnam, one that would also profess a willingness to negotiate. The final draft combined unyielding determination to preserve an independent (i.e. non-communist) South Vietnam with an offer for an extensive food program for all of Vietnam and a US-sponsored billion-dollar development project for the Mekong River region. Johnson loved it. Here was a plan that would satisfy critics on both flanks. More than that, it was a plan that spoke his own language, that expanded the geographic boundaries of the War on Poverty from the domestic front to the underdeveloped world [70].

The essentials of the speech set, the president and a number of advisers read key passages to a variety of leading lawmakers and journalists. Most were pleased with what they heard, especially with a passage that pledged American willingness to engage in 'unconditional discussions' with Hanoi. But one important critic remained skeptical. On 6 April, veteran columnist Walter Lippmann was summoned to the White House for an off-the-record meeting with Johnson, Bundy, and McNamara. It was the second such meeting in the past three weeks, and was part of a Bundy-inspired plan to quiet Lippmann's apprehension by making him feel like his views were welcome in the administration. In a memorandum to Johnson before the meeting, Bundy restated that rationale. 'It would be perfectly proper,' he wrote, 'to show the current draft of your speech to Walter Lippmann and get his opinion. A part of our purpose, after all, is to plug his guns, and he can tell us better than anyone to what degree we have done so.'

Merely showing Lippmann the speech would not be enough, Bundy stressed. The president should also seek to find out why Lippmann was evidently 'pushing so hard for the notion of a single Vietnam' by advising negotiations without making any demands upon the North Vietnamese. Perhaps, Bundy suggested, negotiations were simply Lippmann's 'idea of a quiet way of giving it [Vietnam] to the Communists.' He suggested that Johnson 'make it clear' that 'when we say we are ready to talk, we do not at all mean that we are ready for a cease-fire. ... Walter needs to understand this, and if he gets it straight from you he is likely to be less objectionable about it.'

According to Lippmann biographer Ronald Steel, the columnist was not persuaded. He listened patiently to an hour-long Johnson monologue ('You say negotiate,' Johnson allegedly said at one point, 'but there is no one over there to negotiate with. So the only thing there is to do is to hang on. And that's what I'm going to do'), and then met privately with Bundy and went over the speech point by point. 'This isn't going to work, Mac,' Lippmann said. 'It's just a disguised demand for capitulation. You've got to give the communists some incentive to negotiate.' 'Like what?' Bundy asked. 'Like an unconditional cease-fire,' Lippmann replied. Bundy pondered the idea, then said he would see what he could do. The two men went back and forth for another hour about the feasibility of a cease-fire and negotiations before Bundy reluctantly let the elder man go [188].

Lippmann may have had serious doubts about the speech and its promises, but he was virtually alone. When Johnson delivered it the next day at Johns Hopkins University in Baltimore, it was immediately hailed as the most important foreign policy speech of his presidency and widely perceived as demonstrating the administration's restraint and willingness to negotiate [*Doc. 19*]. The *New York Times* reversed its previous editorial criticism and lauded the president for 'an American policy ... in which the country can take pride.' White House mail was overwhelmingly positive. Congressional critics, among them William Fulbright, Frank Church, and Mike Mansfield, praised Johnson's openness to negotiations and the offer of economic aid to North Vietnam. And U Thant, in a letter to Johnson the next day, predicted that the speech 'will mark a turning point in the long-standing Vietnam conflict.' The secretary-general based this prediction on one key passage: 'I regard your indication of a readiness to enter into "unconditional discussions" as both constructive and statesmanlike. I feel sure that it will prove to be very helpful' [204].

Like so many others who heard the speech, Thant had misread the 'unconditional discussions' pledge. Neither Johnson nor his top advisers

1. Ho Chi Minh (1890–1969) – leading Vietnamese revolutionary and president of the Democratic Republic of Vietnam from 1945 until his death.
Source: Peter Newark's Military Pictures

2. Communist Viet Minh troops wearing camouflage ready for combat against the French, 20 January 1951.
Source: Peter Newark's Military Pictures

3. French and Vietnam troops recover supplies parachuted into North-West Indochina, 6 December 1952.
Source: Peter Newark's Military Pictures

4. Ngo Dinh Diem (1901–1963) – President of the Republic of (South) Vietnam,
June 1954 to November 1963.
Source: Popperfoto

5. President John F. Kennedy and Secretary of Defence Robert S. McNamara, April 1963.
Source: U S Army Photograph/courtesy John F. Kennedy Library, Boston

6. President Lyndon B. Johnson and British Prime Minister Harold Wilson in Washington, April 1965.
Source: Yoichi R. Okamoto, LBJ Library Collection

7. US troops signal helicopter landing zone in combat area, 1965.
Source: Peter Newark's Military Pictures

intended it to be a fundamental departure from previous policy. Talk was cheap. The offer was for unconditional discussions, not negotiations, and it signified only a willingness to talk, not necessarily to reach an agreement. A careful listener might have detected the administration's attitude in the way the pledge was introduced. 'We have stated this position over and over again, fifty times and more, to friend and foe alike,' read the sentence preceding it.

The administration's determination to pursue a military solution conditioned its evaluation of the North Vietnamese response to the Johns Hopkins speech. Issued by Pham Van Dong on 8 April, the response took the form of a four-point program intended to serve as the basis for negotiations with the United States. Specifically, the plan called for the withdrawal of American military personnel from South Vietnam, the termination of hostile actions against the North, the formation of a coalition government in Saigon 'in accordance with the program of the NLF,' and the peaceful reunification of Vietnam without any foreign interference. The points should be regarded, Dong said, as a 'basis for the soundest political settlement' of the war [*Doc. 20*].

For Johnson and his inner circle the Hanoi program was wholly unacceptable, so much so that they chose not to respond to it. But some in the administration took a different view, arguing that the United States should at least explore the precise meaning of Pham Van Dong's statement. Speechwriter Richard Goodwin, for example, conceded that some aspects of the statement were unacceptable but noted that the North Vietnamese premier did not explicitly stipulate American acceptance of each point prior to opening negotiations. Perhaps Hanoi saw them as a 'statement of ultimate objectives' and as a way to reassure the NLF, Goodwin suggested, not as preconditions designed to kill the prospect of talks. Similarly, a NSC assessment concluded, 'If we choose to make them so, Pham Van Dong's proposals could provide the basis for a negotiating dialogue.' Even McGeorge Bundy, after describing North Vietnam's response as 'quite unacceptable to us,' acknowledged that the Hanoi message had referred to the four points as 'a basis for discussions' and that he and acting CIA director Ray Cline, as well as former ambassador to Moscow Llewellyn Thompson, all agreed that there existed 'at least a hint of real interest from Hanoi in eventual discussions' [36; 107].

## FORTY-FOUR BATTALIONS

Even as he was writing those words, however, Bundy and other top officials were in the midst of a series of policy discussions that were to escalate further the US commitment to the war. Pressure for such action had been building since mid-March, when General Harold K. Johnson, the army chief of staff, returned from a fact-finding mission to Saigon and urged the deployment of a full American army division to reinforce ARVN units in the field. The president and McNamara were sympathetic, despite the objections of Ambassador Taylor, who feared that the introduction of more American ground troops could encourage the ARVN forces to lie down on the job and would make it look like the United States was assuming France's colonial role. General William Westmoreland, commander of American forces in Vietnam, went a step further than General Johnson, asking for the immediate dispatch of two divisions to South Vietnam and for permission to use them in offensive operations in the Central Highlands. And the JCS, long impatient with the administration's caution and anxious to take full command of the fighting, asked for three US divisions and a South Korean one.

Johnson compromised. He did not grant the Westmoreland and JCS requests but he authorized the deployment of two marine battalions plus an air squadron and 18,000–20,000 support troops. Though the marines were ordered to remain in enclaves around air bases in the South, they were authorized to engage in offensive operations within 50 miles of their base area. In the weeks that followed, LBJ approved the dispatch of additional units. By mid-May, the total number of American forces in Vietnam had risen to 47,000 and was still climbing to the new ceiling of 82,000.

Despite the steady expansion of US military action since February, the military situation grew steadily worse as spring turned into summer. In North Vietnam, the main effect of the new show of American muscle was to remove the constraints that had previously kept the DRV from sending sizable numbers of its own combat units below the 17th parallel, and to strengthen Hanoi's ties to China and the Soviet Union [*Doc. 21*]. In April, Ho Chi Minh met secretly with Mao Zedong in Beijing and received assurances that China would provide whatever material support the DRV needed. Mao also said he was prepared to send Chinese support troops. By May, these were ready to move. Some Politburo members in Hanoi were intensely hostile to the idea of welcoming Chinese soldiers on to Vietnamese soil, but eventually a compromise was reached that limited what the Chinese could build. In addition, the Chinese offered a concession: North Vietnamese pilots could take off and land from runways on China's side of the border, thus protecting them from hot pursuit by US pilots. By June, Chinese ground-to-air missile, anti-aircraft artillery, minesweeping, engineering, logistics, and railroad units were in North Vietnam.

Soviet assistance to Hanoi and the NLF also increased in these months. In late April 1965, the staff of the NLF's permanent mission in Moscow arrived in the city, to considerable fanfare. On 3 June Premier Kosygin received Dang Quang Minh, the head of the mission, and told him the USSR attached great importance to its relations with the Front. Two days later, a delegation from Hanoi arrived in Moscow for high-level meetings. The talks lasted until 10 July and yielded an agreement for increased Soviet economic and military assistance to North Vietnam. Kremlin leaders had no desire to see a large-scale war in Vietnam, one that might result in a major Cold War crisis, and they made clear there were limits to what Ho Chi Minh's government could expect to receive. But they felt compelled to bolster an ally in need, and to match Chinese assistance with aid of its own [66].

In South Vietnam, meanwhile, the ARVN was reeling. Desertion rates among draftees at induction centers topped 50 percent. When the Vietcong launched a major offensive in mid-May it found little resistance. During the ensuing weeks, several ARVN battalions were decimated in a series of bloody engagements. The defeats reinforced General Westmoreland's already ingrained doubts about the ARVN's capabilities. By early June he had concluded that only major US ground forces could avert disaster in Vietnam.

No doubt Westmoreland based that conclusion partly on the similarly dismal political situation. Phan Huy Quat's government, which had been formed in February and which had never had widespread support, grew more and more weak as the spring progressed. After Quat tried to shake up his cabinet in May, another crisis developed and the so-called Young Turks, led by Air Marshal Nguyen Cao Ky and General Nguyen Van Thieu, succeeded in dissolving the Quat government and assuming power. With Ky becoming prime minister and Quat assuming the title of president, the veneer of civilian rule in South Vietnam was completely stripped away. Policy-makers in Washington were pleased by the new leadership's professed commitment to the war effort, but they had little faith in its capabilities. The Ky–Thieu team 'seemed to all of us the bottom of the barrel,' William Bundy later recalled, 'absolutely the bottom of the barrel.'

It is not surprising, therefore, that Bundy and other officials were sympathetic when Westmoreland in June advocated a massive injection of US troops and the adoption of a new strategy in the field. In a 7 June cable he warned of impending catastrophe in the war effort unless nineteen more American battalions be added to the thirteen already committed to South Vietnam. Westmoreland conceded that such a deployment meant a dramatic and open-ended expansion of American military involvement, but he insisted it was the only way to stabilize the situation. He raised the request to 44 battalions two weeks later, and asked for permission to abandon the enclave strategy for an aggressive, offensive one [144 *III*].

Several mid-level American officials worked to head off the slide into major war. Undersecretary of State George Ball wrote several lengthy memos in the spring and early summer, some of them more penetrating than others, urging a halt in the escalation and a move toward negotiations.

But it was too late. The momentum toward major war had become too strong. In July 1965, despite last-minute warnings from George Ball, Mike Mansfield, William Fulbright, and Democratic Party elder Clark Clifford, Johnson approved the immediate deployment of an additional 50,000 US troops and privately agreed to send another 50,000 before the end of the year [*Doc. 22*]. He also authorized Westmoreland to adopt an offensive, search-and-destroy strategy and to increase dramatically the bombing of North Vietnam.

For many Americans, it all seemed to have happened too fast. Had not Lyndon Johnson campaigned as the peace president, as the man who would keep America out of another Asian land war? What had happened? To some degree Americans shocked by the new developments had to blame themselves – any reasonably attentive reader of one of the major American newspapers over the previous months would have known that the crisis was deepening. More important, however, the Johnson administration had worked hard throughout the spring to keep the public in the dark as much as possible. Key decisions were kept secret. Skeptics in the press and in Congress were leaned on to come out in support of the policy or at least keep their reservations quiet. Administration spokesmen assured any and all that the new measures were really a substitute for escalation rather than escalation itself.

There was no hiding it any longer. Vietnam had become an American war.

# CHAPTER SIX

## AN AVOIDABLE WAR?

It was an ignominious end for the United States in Vietnam. On 1 May 1975, NLF soldiers triumphantly ran up their flag in Saigon. Not long before, the South Vietnamese government had surrendered unconditionally, and US President Gerald Ford had declared that the Vietnam War was 'finished as far as the United States is concerned.' It was two years since the last American ground forces had left the country (following the January 1973 Paris Peace Accords), and it marked the end of the Second Indochina War.

Like all large-scale wars, this one exacted heavy costs on all sides. Foremost among these was the staggering number of deaths, especially among Vietnamese (between three and four million Vietnamese lost their lives), and the utter destruction of much of the country of Vietnam and large portions of Laos and Cambodia. In the United States, the war caused deep social divisions, fostered a destructive cynicism about government claims and actions that persists to this day, and exacted staggering short-term and long-term economic costs. In terms of foreign affairs, the administration's obsession with Vietnam after mid-1965 caused it to neglect other vital foreign policy issues, including relations with Latin America, Europe, and the Middle East, as well as the difficult frictions between rich and poor nations [33]. What is more, the war was largely responsible for the lack of progress in East–West relations in the Johnson years. Without the conflict in Vietnam, Soviet-American *détente* might well have come in the mid-1960s, with potentially longer-lasting effects than the version that came later [48].

That the American decision for war in 1965 was the wrong decision is today taken as axiomatic by a large majority of both lay observers and scholars, who see the US intervention as, at best, a failure and a mistake, and at worst a crime. 'We were wrong, terribly wrong,' the former secretary of defense Robert McNamara, one of the architects of the escalation, intoned in his 1995 memoirs [132]. Critics vilified McNamara for taking three decades to speak out, but virtually no one questioned the veracity of his assertion.

So might the war have been avoided? Go back far enough and the answer is obviously yes. In the United States, the decision in 1950 to provide major assistance to the French war effort had important long-term implications, but it did not make inevitable an American war fifteen years later. Nor did the Eisenhower administration's decision in 1954 to create and sustain a non-communist bastion in southern Vietnam do so, key though that development was. Some authors have claimed that Kennedy's move in the fall of 1961 to send significantly more US advisers to South Vietnam was the point of no return, but they do not convince, and neither do those who say that the key moment was the decision to facilitate a coup against Ngo Dinh Diem in November 1963.

In Vietnam, Diem's repressive policies did much to destabilize South Vietnam in the period 1954–63, but here again the end result need not have been a major war. The same goes for his determination – supported by Washington – to bypass the 1956 elections for reunification called for in the Geneva Accords. The Hanoi government, meanwhile, made a series of policy choices in the earlier period that, though momentous, were not determinative: here one thinks, for example, of the move in 1959 to resume military activity in the South, and the action by the Ninth Plenum of the Vietnamese Workers' Party in December 1963 to increase aid to the Vietcong.

Certainly, understanding the Vietnam War means understanding this earlier history of US–Vietnamese relations, a history going back to at least World War II. The policy decisions of Roosevelt, Truman, Eisenhower, and Kennedy, as well as those of their counterparts in Saigon and Hanoi, laid the foundation for the large-scale war that broke out in 1965. But the question to be addressed here, that of inevitability, really hinges on whether there existed a genuine opportunity for a non-military solution in the critical months of 1964–65. And for the answer we must look predominately to the deliberations in Washington. Hanoi's actions in the period obviously mattered, but its leaders, though firmly committed to achieving reunification of Vietnam under their control, were not keen on a major expansion of the fighting; indeed, they hoped very much to avoid it, and were content to bide their time. In South Vietnam, meanwhile, apathy and war weariness were rampant, and there were persistent rumors that even some senior government officials wanted an end to the struggle through a deal with the NLF or Hanoi; few wanted an expansion of the fighting. The decision for major war in Vietnam, it can safely be said, was above all an American decision.

Contemporaneous critics of the war, writing while the decisions were being made, were convinced that alternatives existed, and they blasted the Johnson administration for rejecting opportunities for a diplomatic solution. Senior officials, too, perceived that they had a very real choice about which way to go: as Secretary of State Dean Rusk said at a top-level meeting at Camp David on 10 March 1965, in words that had been uttered numerous times in policy discussions in the months prior, the United States could opt for either 'escalation or negotiation.'

Curiously, however, most later scholars implicitly or explicitly rejected that a real choice existed for American decision-makers in 1964–65. These authors often differed dramatically on many issues pertaining to the war, but on this much they agreed: that after the middle or latter part of 1964, if not earlier, a fundamental reorientation in US policy, though certainly preferable in hindsight, is virtually impossible to imagine. They described an escalation process that was essentially an inevitable outcome of the domestic and international climate of the time. More than that, almost all of these authors implied that the president was justified in believing that each escalation might provide the critical increment – after all, everyone else thought so.

The evidence does not support this view. There were in fact numerous influential voices inside and outside the government, inside and outside the United States, who rejected the administration's claim that maintaining an independent, non-communist South Vietnam was imperative. The list of those in the United States who believed by the start of 1965 that the objective was either unattainable or unimportant, or both, included the Senate Democratic leadership of Majority Leader Mike Mansfield, Foreign Relations Committee chairman J. William Fulbright, and Armed Services Committee chairman Richard Russell, as well as perhaps two dozen other Senate Democrats. It also included Vice-President Hubert H. Humphrey. Outside the government, those who argued likewise included columnists Walter Lippmann, Joseph Kraft, and Drew Pearson and newspapers across the country, including the *New York Times* and the *Washington Post*. In the larger public opinion, no Cold War Consensus existed that demanded a staunch US commitment to South Vietnam. As late as March 1965, polls of the public and Congress revealed widespread antipathy for the introduction of US ground troops into the conflict, and broad support for negotiations.

In the international community, meanwhile, America was largely isolated on Vietnam by the beginning of 1965. By then the list of opponents of Americanization had grown to include virtually every government in Western Europe, as well as those in Ottawa and Tokyo, and leading statesmen such as the UN secretary-general, U Thant, and the French president, Charles de Gaulle. Sympathetic to Washington's plight in some cases, these international voices nevertheless doubted that the war could be won or that it was necessary even to try. The essential prerequisite for any successful outcome to the struggle – a stable Saigon government enjoying reasonably broad-based popular support – was not merely absent but further away than ever from becoming reality. A stepped-up American military effort could probably help stabilize the situation on the battlefield but could not rectify the fundamental problem, the unwillingness of the mass of southerners to fight for the regime. If anything, a larger American presence in the

South would exacerbate the problem by making the regime seem more like a puppet than ever before. Far better, therefore, for Washington to seek a negotiated disengagement from the conflict.

The American government's reaction to these calls for negotiations reveals a great deal about US policy-making in the Kennedy and Johnson periods. As we have seen, US officials feared the potential impact of such efforts on support for the war in Saigon and in the international community, and they made continuous attempts to convince the proponents of a political solution either to alter their stance or at least to stay silent on the issue, with mixed success.

Thus the importance to our story of Dean Rusk's State Department. As America's chief diplomat it was Rusk's business to seek political solutions to international conflicts, to think imaginatively about ways to get his country out of a mess in Vietnam with a minimum of bloodshed and a minimum loss of prestige. But Rusk, doggedly committed to preserving the US commitment to Saigon, engaged in little such thinking. He and his colleagues refused to consider following the advice and heeding the warnings of this formidable group of foreign and domestic Cassandras. That is the ultimate tragedy, for these proponents of negotiations, whatever their biases and motivations, understood the nature of the Vietnam conflict and correctly predicted the dire outcome of a continued application of American policy. As the decade progressed and American troop levels – and casualties – grew, more and more individuals came to share their views.

To be sure, the prescience of, say, a Mansfield memorandum, or a Lippmann column, or a de Gaulle press release, is considerably more clear today than it was in 1964 or 1965. Moreover, that prescience was not always accompanied by determined effort. In many instances, allied leaders and domestic observers who foresaw a great calamity ahead should escalation occur failed to work hard to keep it from happening. Indeed, it was precisely those domestic and foreign voices that would have had the greatest potential impact on top officials that were the most reticent about speaking out. Thus while the de Gaulle government in Paris forcefully disputed the US position at every turn, the more important American ally in London consistently refrained from doing so, despite the fact that officials there largely shared the French leader's views. And even de Gaulle cannot be considered an agitator *per se* on negotiations in 1963–65; for the most part, he was content to state his views and then watch to see what the Americans chose to do. In the United States Senate, key players – Majority Leader Mansfield and Foreign Relations Committee chairman Fulbright, for example – too often took care to keep their concerns private and even to do the administration's bidding on occasion. Undersecretary of State George Ball's opposition to an Americanized war was genuine and heartfelt, but it is less clear that he expended great effort to try to head it off.

The same general point could be made about the leaders in North Vietnam. Hanoi officials had always, since the days of the Geneva Conference in 1954, sought to avert a large-scale American military intervention in Vietnam – this objective ranked second only to the overriding quest for reunification of the country under their control. Right up to the spring of 1965, they hoped to prevent such an eventuality, hoped their US counterparts would conclude that the political and military mess in the South made de-escalation the only option. They did not, however, do much to push the Americans to this desired result. Fearful of a repeat of Geneva – they fared worse at that conference than their military position suggested they should – and continually underestimating Lyndon Johnson's commitment to a military solution, DRV leaders stayed largely quiet on the negotiations issue in the key months leading up to war. They held better diplomatic cards than the Americans, but arguably played their hand no better.

Yet if the passage of a quarter century grants us the luxury of hindsight, and if the opponents of war too often failed to really press their case, the fact remains that Lyndon Johnson had a legitimate choice on which way to proceed in Vietnam, a choice laid out *at the time* by both the opponents and proponents of negotiations. This makes the decision for war more difficult to explain than many studies would have one believe, as does the fact that senior US officials shared many of the same judgments as their detractors about the state of the war in Vietnam and the prospects for a turn-around. Lyndon Johnson and his top foreign policy aides were, for the most part, gloomy realists on Vietnam, well aware of the problems in the war effort and the obstacles in the way of significant improvement. They talked confidently about what Operation Rolling Thunder could achieve, but privately they were skeptical that the bombing would cause Hanoi to call it quits or that it would do much to help the politico-military problems in the South. Even as they sent the first contingent of US ground forces, senior officials understood that it would bring resentment from many South Vietnamese, including those in leadership positions, and generate charges of 'colonialism' from elsewhere in Asia and around the world. As for the quality of the Saigon government, US policy-makers were no less dubious than their critics; they knew it had less popular support than ever, that it was characterized by in-fighting and incompetence, and that at least some of its members were flirting with the idea of seeking an early negotiated settlement of the conflict.

Even on the core question of whether the outcome in Vietnam really mattered to US security, many policy-makers were prepared to see the logic of the skeptics' position – that defeat in Vietnam need not be a major blow, particularly if the loss happened because of the perceived apathy or ineptitude of the South Vietnamese themselves. Officials understood that the historic Sino-Vietnamese friction and the emerging Sino-Soviet split lessened the possibility that Beijing would expand its influence widely in the wake of a Saigon defeat. They grasped that the conditions that made Vietnam so ripe for a communist take-over did not exist in many other nations in the region. The Soviet Union, many analysts were confident, would want to continue steps toward improved relations with the United States regardless of the outcome in Vietnam.

No doubt a presidential decision to seek negotiations from a less-than-optimal military position would have exacted a political price at home. Conservative lawmakers and journalists would have raised the specter of another Manchuria, another Munich, another 'loss of China.' But the price would not have been an exorbitant one. Johnson had just won a massive election victory, and he possessed huge Democratic majorities in both houses of Congress. His public approval ratings had never been higher. Vice-President Humphrey spoke well to this point in early 1965 in registering opposition to escalation. The American people, he warned the president in mid-February, could not be expected to support for long a war few of them understood. The stakes were not clear, and a wider war could mean major political trouble for the administration. Far better, Humphrey argued, to decrease American involvement in the war, especially now, with the administration so strong at home. Nineteen-sixty-five, he wrote, 'is the year of minimum political risk for the Johnson administration,' when it need no longer be 'preoccupied with the repercussions from the Republican Right' [*Doc. 18*].

Consider Humphrey's credentials in making these claims. Here was a man whose understanding of Democratic precinct politics across the nation was every bit as authoritative as that of Lyndon Johnson. Humphrey was as steeped in the politics and ideology of the Cold War as any Democrat before or since. He could even be regarded as one of the architects of the postwar anti-communist doctrine, with his early attacks on communist-led unions. No one needed to educate him on the various problems, domestic and external, that might follow from incurring the charge of 'losing' a country to communism. Yet here we find Humphrey in February 1965, in an extraordinarily prescient memorandum penned just as the war was being Americanized, telling LBJ that 1965 was the best time to incur these risks and that the political risks of escalation were far greater.

Some authors, such as Leslie H. Gelb and Richard K. Betts, have nevertheless contended that it is wrong to criticize Johnson and his predecessors for not getting out of Vietnam since 'the mainstream of the American political system never asked them to' [72]. A debatable assertion – in early 1965 key elements in that system were urging precisely that, albeit circumspectly – this is in any event defining presidential leadership too narrowly. Given repeated warnings of serious trouble and poor prospects, the presidents had a duty to ascertain the facts, present them to the American people, and persuade them to cut their losses. This was true of Eisenhower and Kennedy, and it was true of Johnson. From his ascension to the presidency until well into 1965, Johnson could have negotiated a withdrawal after telling the public that the United States could no longer defend militarily a government so demonstrably unwilling to do its part in the struggle. He could have drawn a distinction between communist aggression against another country and the civil war in Vietnam. He could have argued that the best American response to communism around the world would be to build a Great Society at home and maintain an economy strong enough to help allies around the globe. But Johnson did not. He chose what he believed to be the path of least political resistance and escalated the war. He failed to do what great political leaders must do, which is to rise to the occasion and lead and educate their constituents. As a result, the American people did not get the Vietnam policy they deserved.

Precisely what would have resulted from negotiations in 1963 or 1964 or 1965 is hard to determine, but the indications are strong that through February 1965, at least, the DRV would have accepted a Geneva conference leading to an independent, neutral government in Saigon that included elements of the NLF. Others, too, wanted such a result. The two major European powers at Geneva also supported reconvening the meeting, much to Washington's chagrin. In the view of both the French and the British, Washington faced a set of poor choices in Vietnam. A serious attempt at negotiations made good sense to them, if only because the military outlook for the US/RVN side was so grim. Officials in Paris and London felt confident, as did U Thant and others in the international community, that communist peace terms at a conference could be packaged in such a way as to give the Americans a reasonably graceful exit from Vietnam.

What about the two leading communist powers? For the Soviet Union, a large-scale war in Vietnam would be the wrong war in the wrong place at the wrong time. The prospects for Soviet–American *détente* would diminish, and the Kremlin would be asked to honor its commitment to the DRV by raising its level of material and rhetorical support. Furthermore, what if the Chinese were drawn into such a war? Would that compel Moscow to abide by the 1950 Sino-Soviet treaty and come in also? Even if not, would Chinese intervention result in *de facto* Beijing control of Indochina? The possibilities made Brezhnev and Kosygin and their colleagues shudder, and exposed their problem: in order to deter a world conflagration they had to constrain the North Vietnamese, but their need to compete with Beijing for the affection of Asian nationalists compelled them nevertheless to pledge assistance to Hanoi. Kremlin leaders thus saw real advantages in a great-power conference, one that would allow for a face-saving American disengagement and put Hanoi in a strong position to win eventual control of a reunified Vietnam.

As for China, its leadership early in 1965 was not keen on going to Geneva – it much preferred to see the American-sponsored regime continue to flounder – but neither was it prepared to rule it out. Through the start of Rolling Thunder Chinese leaders were careful to say merely that a great-power meeting on the war was unnecessary, not that they would never attend one. For that matter, the Chinese had reasons of their own to look with favor on a conference, if only as an alternative to major war. Notwithstanding their glee at Washington's troubles in Vietnam, and their scathing public denunciations of US policy, they were not eager for a direct military confrontation with the United States. Nor was an increased American involvement the only thing that concerned the Beijing leadership; it also had to worry about the prospect of a revived Soviet influence on China's Southeast Asian border, influence certain only to increase in the event of a major war since Moscow could offer the DRV much more in the way of economic and military assistance than China could.

In the international community, then, the constellation of forces in early 1965 suggested the opportunity for fashioning a political settlement that could allow the United States to escape a situation that all could agree was a mess with its prestige largely intact. At home, a negotiated withdrawal would have won the support of powerful voices in elite public opinion, including Johnson's own Democratic leadership in Congress. But the president and his men nevertheless chose war. Their reasoning was complex, but primarily they acted not out of tangible geopolitical concerns or moral attachment to the South Vietnamese, but out of fear of embarrassment – to the United States and the Democratic Party and, above all, to themselves personally. Time and again over the years they had publicly vowed American steadfastness in the struggle, had declared the outcome in Vietnam to be crucial to US security, and they were loathe to change their tune now. So they charged ahead, desperate to avoid the taint of failure.

For the proponents of a negotiated settlement, the July 1965 decisions were dramatic proof of the failure of their efforts to shift the struggle from the military to the political arena. Beginning with Charles de Gaulle's neutralization push in the late summer and fall of 1963, these advocates had relentlessly pressed their case that the administrations in Washington misunderstood the nature of the struggle and that, at any rate, a lasting military victory for the United States could never be achieved. The best solution, therefore, was a political settlement and an American withdrawal, even if the end result would be a communist Vietnam. Though their arguments had widespread support – among America's allies, among many in Vietnam, and among important constituencies in the United States – they failed to convince those who really mattered: policy-makers in Washington. The result was a tragedy, for Lyndon Johnson, for the United States, and for the people of Vietnam.

# PART FOUR    DOCUMENTS

*The founding of Doc-Lap Dong Minh Hoi (Vietminh) in the village of Pac
Bo, near the Sino-Vietnamese border, in June 1941. Ho calls for an independence struggle against Japan and France.*

Elders! Prominent personalities! Intellectuals, peasants, workers, traders,
and soldiers! Dear compatriots!

Since the French were defeated by the Germans, their forces have been
completely disintegrated, However, with regard to our people, they continue to plunder us pitilessly, suck all our blood, and carry out a barbarous
policy of all-out terrorism and massacre. Concerning their foreign policy,
they bow their heads and kneel down, shamelessly cutting our land for
Siam; without a single word of protest, they heartlessly offer our interests to
Japan. As a result, our people suffer under a double yoke: they serve not
only as buffaloes and horses to the French invaders but also as slaves to the
Japanese plunderers. Alas! What sin have our people committed to be
doomed to such a wretched plight!

Now, the opportunity has come for our liberation. France itself is unable
to dominate our country. As to the Japanese, on the one hand they are
bogged in China, on the other, they are hamstrung by the British and American forces, and certainly cannot use all their forces to contend with us. If
our entire people are united and single-minded, we are certainly able to
smash the picked French and Japanese armies.

Some hundreds of years ago, when our country was endangered by the
Mongolian invasion, our elders under the Tran dynasty rose up indignantly
and called on their sons and daughters throughout the country to rise as
one in order to kill the enemy. Finally they saved their people from danger,
and their good name will be carried into posterity for all time. The elders
and prominent personalities of our country should follow the example set
by our forefathers in the glorious task of national salvation.

Rich people, soldiers, workers, peasants, intellectuals, employees, traders,
youth, and women who warmly love your country! At present time national
liberation is the most important problem. Let us unite together! As one
mind and strength we shall overthrow the Japanese and French and their
jackals in order to save people from the situation between boiling water and
burning heat.

Dear compatriots!

National Salvation is the common cause to the whole of our people.
Every Vietnamese must take part in it. He who has money will contribute
his money, he who has strength will contribute his strength, he who has
talent will contribute his talent. I pledge to use all my modest abilities to
follow you, and am ready for the last sacrifice.

Revolutionary fighters!

The hour has struck! Raise aloft the insurrectionary banner and guide the people throughout the country to overthrow the Japanese and French! The sacred call of the fatherland is resounding in your ears; the blood of our heroic predecessors who sacrificed their lives is stirring in your hearts! The fighting spirit of the people is displayed everywhere before you! Let us rise up quickly! Compatriots throughout the country, rise up quickly! United with each other, unify your action to overthrow the Japanese and the French. Victory to Vietnam's Revolution!

Victory to the World's Revolution!

Ho Chi Minh, *Selected Works*, 4 vols, Hanoi: Foreign Languages Publishing House, 1960–62, II, pp. 151–4.

DOCUMENT 2   **THE VIETNAMESE DECLARATION OF INDEPENDENCE, SEPTEMBER 1945**

*Ho Chi Minh declares Vietnam to be independent of France, in Hanoi's Ba Dinh square on 2 September 1945.*

All men are created equal; they are endowed by their Creator with certain unalienable Rights; among these are Life, Liberty, and the pursuit of Happiness.

This immortal statement was made in the Declaration of Independence of the United States of America in 1776. In a broader sense, this means: All the peoples on the earth are equal from birth, all the peoples have a right to live, to be happy and free.

The Declaration of the French Revolution made in 1791 on the Rights of Man and the Citizen also states: 'All men are born free and with equal rights, and must always remain free and have equal rights.'

Those are undeniable truths.

Nevertheless, for more than eighty years, the French imperialists, abusing the standard of Liberty, Equality, and Fraternity, have violated our Fatherland and oppressed our fellow citizens. They have acted contrary to the ideals of humanity and justice.

In the field of politics, they have deprived our people of every democratic liberty.

They have enforced inhuman laws; they have set up three distinct political regimes in the North, the Center, and the South of Viet-Nam in order to wreck our national unity and prevent our people from being united.

They have built more prisons than schools. They have mercilessly slain our patriots; they have drowned our uprisings in rivers of blood.

They have fettered public opinion; they have practiced obscurantism against our people.

To weaken our race they have forced us to use opium and alcohol.

In the field of economics, they have fleeced us to the backbone, impoverished our people and devastated our land.

They have robbed us of our rice fields, our mines, our forests, and our raw materials. They have monopolized the issuing of bank notes and the export trade.

They have invented numerous unjustifiable taxes and reduced our people, especially our peasantry, to a state of extreme poverty.

They have hampered the prospering of our national bourgeoisie; they have mercilessly exploited our workers.

In the autumn of 1940, when the Japanese fascists violated Indochina's territory to establish new bases in their fight against the Allies, the French imperialists went down on their bended knees and handed over our country to them.

Thus, from that date, our people were subjected to the double yoke of the French and the Japanese. Their sufferings and miseries increased. The result was that, from the end of last year to the beginning of this year, from Quang Tri Province to the North of Viet-Nam, more than two million of our fellow citizens died from starvation. On March 9 [1945], the French troops were disarmed by the Japanese. The French colonialists either fled or surrendered, showing that not only were they incapable of 'protecting' us, but that, in the span of five years, they had twice sold our country to the Japanese.

On several occasions before March 9, the Viet Minh League urged the French to ally themselves with it against the Japanese. Instead of agreeing to this proposal, the French colonialists so intensified their terrorist activities against the Viet Minh members that before fleeing they massacred a great number of our political prisoners detained at Yen Bay and Cao Bang.

Notwithstanding all this, our fellow citizens have always manifested toward the French a tolerant and humane attitude. Even after the Japanese *Putsch* of March, 1945, the Viet Minh League helped many Frenchmen to cross the frontier, rescued some of them from Japanese jails, and protected French lives and property.

From the autumn of 1940, our country had in fact ceased to be a French colony and had become a Japanese possession.

After the Japanese had surrendered to the Allies, our whole people rose to regain our national sovereignty and to found the Democratic Republic of Viet-Nam.

The truth is that we have wrested our independence from the Japanese and not from the French.

The French have fled, the Japanese have capitulated, Emperor Bao Dai has abdicated. Our people have broken the chains which for nearly a century have fettered them and have won independence for the Fatherland. Our people at the same time have overthrown the monarchic regime that has reigned supreme for dozens of centuries. In its place has been established the present Democratic Republic.

For these reasons, we, members of the Provisional Government, representing the whole Vietnamese people, declare that from now on we break off all relations of a colonial character with France; we repeal all the international obligation that France has so far subscribed to on behalf of Viet-Nam, and we abolish all the special rights the French have unlawfully acquired in our Fatherland.

The whole Vietnamese people, animated by a common purpose, are determined to fight to the bitter end against any attempt by the French colonialists to reconquer their country.

We are convinced that the Allied nations, which at Teheran and San Francisco have acknowledged the principles of self-determination and equality of nations, will not refuse to acknowledge the independence of Viet-Nam.

A people who have courageously opposed French domination for more than eighty years, a people who have fought side by side with the Allies against the fascists during these last years, such a people must be free and independent.

For these reasons, we, members of the Provisional Government of the Democratic Republic of Viet-Nam, solemnly declare to the world that Viet-Nam has the right to be a free and independent country – and in fact it is so already. The entire Vietnamese people are determined to mobilize all their physical and mental strength, to sacrifice their lives and property in order to safeguard their independence and liberty.

Ho Chi Minh, *Selected Works*, 4 vols, Hanoi: Foreign Languages Publishing House, 1960–62, III, pp. 17–21.

---

DOCUMENT 3   **HO CHI MINH COURTS US SUPPORT, OCTOBER 1945**

*Ho Chi Minh's letter to Secretary of State James F. Byrnes seeking support for the people of Vietnam, 22 October 1945.*

Excellency: The situation in South Vietnam has reached its critical stage, and calls for immediate interference on the part of the United Nations. I wish by the present letter to bring your excellency some more light on the case of Vietnam which has come for the last three weeks into the international limelight. ...

After 80 years of French oppression and unsuccessful though obstinate Vietnamese resistance, we at last saw France defeated in Europe, then her betrayal of the Allies successively on behalf of Germany and of Japan. Though the odds were at that time against the Allies, the Vietnamese, leaving aside all differences in political opinion, united in the Vietminh League and started on a ruthless fight against the Japanese. Meanwhile, the Atlantic Charter was concluded, defining the war aims of the Allies and laying the foundation of peace-work. The noble principles of international justice and equality of status laid down in that charter strongly appealed to the Vietnamese and contributed in making of the Vietminh resistance in the war zone a nation-wide anti-Japanese movement which found a powerful echo in the democratic aspirations of the people. The Atlantic Charter was looked upon as the foundation of future Vietnam. A nation-building program was drafted which was later found in keeping with San Francisco Charter and which has been fully carried out these last years: continuous fight against the Japenese bringing about the recovery of national independence on August 19th, voluntary abdication of Ex-Emperor Baodai, establishment of the Democratic Republic of Vietnam, assistance given to the Allies Nations in the disarmament of the Japanese, appointment of a provisional Government whose mission was to carry out the Atlantic and San Francisco Charters and have them carried out by other nations.

As a matter of fact, the carrying out of the Atlantic and San Francisco Charters implies the eradication of imperialism and all forms of colonial oppression. This was unfortunately contrary to the interest of some Frenchmen, and France, to whom the colonists have long concealed the truth on Indochina, instead of entering into peaceable negotiations, resorted to an aggressive invasion with all the means at the command of a modern nation. Moreover, having persuaded the British that the Vietnamese are wishing for a return of the French rule, they obtained, first from the British command in Southeast Asia, then from London, a tacit recognition of their sovereignty and administrative responsibility as far as South Vietnam is concerned. The British gave to understand that they had agreed to this on the ground that the reestablishment of French administration and, consequently, of Franco-Vietnamese collaboration would help them to speed up the demobilization and the disarmament of the Japanese. But subsequent events will prove the fallacy of the argument. The whole Vietnamese nation rose up as one man against French aggression. The first hours of September 23rd soon developed into real and organized warfare in which losses are heavy on both sides. The bringing in of French important reinforcements on board of the most powerful of their remaining warships will extend the war zone further. As murderous fighting is still going on in Indonesia, and as savage acts on the part of Frenchmen are reported every day, we may expect the flaring up of a general conflagration in the Far-East.

As it is, the situation in South Vietnam calls for immediate interference. The establishment of the Consultative Commission for the Far-East has been enthusiastically welcomed here as the first effective step toward an equitable settlement of the pending problems. The people of Vietnam, which only asks for full independence and for the respect of truth and justice. ...

Gareth Porter, ed., *Vietnam: The Definitive Documentation of Human Decisions*, 2 vols, Stanfordville, NY: E.M. Coleman, 1979, I, pp. 84–5.

DOCUMENT 4   **FRANCO-VIETNAMESE AGREEMENT ON THE INDEPENDENCE OF VIETNAM, MARCH 1946**

*A compromise agreement is reached between French and Vietnamese negotiators in Paris, 6 March 1946.*

1. The French Government recognizes the Vietnamese Republic as a Free State having its own Government, its own Parliament, its own Army and its own Finances, forming part of the Indochinese Federation and of the French Union. In that which concerns the reuniting of the three 'Annamite Regions' [Cochinchina, Annam, Tonkin] the French Government pledges itself to ratify the decisions taken by the populations consulted by referendum.

2. The Vietnamese Government declares itself ready to welcome amicably the French Army when, conforming to international agreements, it relieves the Chinese Troops. A Supplementary Accord, attached to the present Preliminary Agreement, will establish the means by which the relief operations will be carried out.

3. The stipulations formulated above will immediately enter into force. Immediately after the exchange of signatures, each of the High Contracting Parties will take all measures necessary to stop hostilities in the field, to maintain the troops in their respective positions, and to create the favorable atmosphere necessary to the immediate opening of friendly and sincere negotiations. These negotiations will deal particularly with:

   a.  diplomatic relations of Viet-nam with Foreign States
   b.  the future law of Indochina
   c.  French interests, economic and cultural, in Viet-nam.

Hanoi, Saigon or Paris may be chosen as the seat of the conference.

Signed: Sainteny

Signed: Ho-chi Minh
  and Vu Hong Khanh

*The Pentagon Papers: The Defense Department History of Decisionmaking on Vietnam*, The Senator Gravel edition, 5 vols, Boston, 1971–72, I, pp. 18–19.

## DOCUMENT 5    US SUPPORT FOR FRENCH COLONIALISM, MAY 1950

*At a ministerial level meeting in Paris, 8 May 1950, Secretary of State Dean Acheson firmly ties American national interests to achieving a French victory in the war.*

The [French] Foreign Minister and I have just had an exchange of views on the situation in Indochina and are in general agreement both as to the urgency of the situation in that area and as to the necessity for remedial action. We have noted the fact that the problem of meeting the threat to the security of Vietnam, Cambodia, and Laos which now enjoy independence within the French Union is primarily the responsibility of France and the Governments and peoples of Indochina. The United States recognizes that the solution of the Indochina problem depends both upon the restoration of security and upon the development of genuine nationalism and that United States assistance can and should contribute to these major objectives.

    The United States Government, convinced that neither national independence nor democratic evolution exists in any area dominated by Soviet imperialism, considers the situation to be such as to warrant its according economic aid and military equipment to the Associated States of Indochina and to France in order to assist them in restoring stability and permitting these states to pursue their peaceful and democratic development.

*US Department of State Bulletin* 22 (22 May 1950), p. 821.

## DOCUMENT 6    THE DOMINO THEORY, APRIL 1954

*In a press conference on 7 April 1954, President Dwight D. Eisenhower articulates the domino thesis.*

Q. ROBERT RICHARDS, COPLEY PRESS: Mr. President, would you mind commenting on the strategic importance of Indochina to the free world? I think there has been, across the country, some lack of understanding on just what it means to us.

THE PRESIDENT: You have, of course, both the specific and the general when you talk about such things.

First of all, you have the specific value of a locality in its production of materials that the world needs.

Then you have the possibility that many human beings pass under a dictatorship that is inimical to the free world.

Finally, you have broader considerations that might follow what you would call the 'falling domino' principle. You have a row of dominoes set up, you knock over the first one, and what will happen to the last one is the certainty that it will go over very quickly so you could have a beginning of a disintegration that would have the most profound influences.

Now, with respect to the first one, two of the items from this particular area that the world uses are tin and tungsten. They are very important. There are others, of course, the rubber plantations and so on.

Then with respect to more people passing under this domination, Asia, after all, has already lost some 450 million of its peoples to the Communist dictatorship, and we simply can't afford greater losses.

But when we come to the possible sequence of events, the loss of Indochina, of Burma, of Thailand, of the Peninsula, and Indonesia following, now you begin to talk about areas that not only multiply the disadvantages that you would suffer through loss of materials, sources of materials, but now you are talking really about millions and millions and millions of people.

Finally, the geographical position achieved thereby does many things. It turns the so-called island defensive chain of Japan, Formosa, of the Philippines and to the southward; it moves in to threaten Australia and New Zealand.

It takes away, in its economic aspects, that region that Japan must have as a trading area or Japan, in turn, will have only one place in the world to go – that is, toward the Communist areas in order to live.

So, the possible consequences of the loss are just incalculable to the free world.

*Public Papers of the Presidents of the United States: Dwight D. Eisenhower, 1953,*
Washington, DC: Government Printing Office, 1958, pp. 381–90.

DOCUMENT 7    **DIEN BIEN PHU, 1954**

*In 1964, Vo Nguyen Giap reminisces on the paramount significance of the victory at Dien Bien Phu a decade earlier.*

The historic Dien Bien Phu campaign and in general the Winter 1953– Spring 1954 campaign were the greatest victories ever won by our army and people up to the present time. These great victories marked a giant progress, *a momentous change in the evolution of the Resistance War for national salvation put up by our people against the aggressive French imperialists propped up by U.S. interventionists. ...*

*The great Dien Bien Phu victory and the Winter–Spring victories as a whole had a far-reaching influence in the world.*

While the bellicose imperialists were confused and discouraged, the news of the victories won by our army and people on the battlefronts throughout the country, especially the Dien Bien Phu victory, have greatly inspired the progressive people the world over.

The Dien Bien Phu victory was not only a great victory of our people but was regarded by the socialist countries as their own victory. It was regarded as a great victory of the weak and small nations now fighting against imperialism and old and new-colonialism for freedom and independence. Dien Bien Phu has become a pride of the oppressed peoples, a great contribution of our people to the high movement for national liberation which has been surging up powerfully since the end of World War II, and heralded the collapse of the colonial system of imperialism.

Dien Bien Phu was also a great victory of the forces of peace in the world. Without this victory, certainly the Geneva Conference would not be successful and peace could not be re-established in Indo-China. This substantiates all the more clearly that the victory won at Dien Bien Phu and in general the Resistance War put up by our people, and the victorious struggle for liberation waged by the oppressed people against imperialism and colonialism under all forms, played a role of paramount importance in weakening imperialism, thwarting the scheme of aggression and war of the enemy and contributing greatly to the defence of world peace. ...

The aggressive war unleashed by the French imperialists in Indo-China dragged on for eight or nine years. Though they did their best to increase their force to nearly half a million men, sacrificed hundreds of thousands of soldiers, spent in this dirty war 2,688 billion French francs, squandered a great amount of resources, shed a great deal of blood of the French people, changed 20 cabinets in France, 7 high commissars and 8 commanders-in-chief in Indo-China, their aggressive war grew from bad to worse, met defeat after defeat, went from one strategic mistake to another, to end in the great Dien Bien Phu disaster. This is because the war made by the French colonialists was an unjust war. In this war the enemy met with the indomitable spirit of an entire people and therefore, no skilful general – be he Leclerc, De Tassigny, Navarre or any other general – could save the French Expeditionary Corps from defeat. Neither would there be a mighty weapon – cannon, tank or heavy bomber and even U.S. atomic bomb – which could retrieve the situation. On the upshot, if in autumn 1953 and winter 1954, the enemy did not occupy Dien Bien Phu by para-troopers or' if he occupied it and withdrew later without choosing it as the site of a do-or-die battle, sooner or later a Dien Bien Phu would come up, though the time and place might change; and in the end the French and U.S. imperialists would certainly meet with a bitter failure.

Robert J. McMahon, ed., *Major Problems in the History of Vietnam*, Lexington, MA: D.C. Heath, 1990, pp. 122–3.

*The Final Declaration of the Geneva Conference, issued on 21 July 1954.*

1. The Conference takes note of the agreements ending hostilities in Cambodia, Laos, and Vietnam and organizing international control and the supervision of the execution of the provisions of these agreements.

2. The Conference expresses satisfaction at the end of hostilities in Cambodia, Laos, and Vietnam; the Conference expresses its conviction that the execution of the provisions set out in the present declaration and in the agreements of the cessation of hostilities will permit Cambodia, Laos, and Vietnam henceforth to play their part, in full independence and sovereignty, in the peaceful community of nations.

3. The Conference takes note of the declarations made by the Governments of Cambodia and Laos of their intention to adopt measures permitting all citizens to take their place in the national community, in particular by participating in the next general elections, which, in conformity with the constitution of each of these countries, shall take place in the course of the year 1955, by secret ballot and in conditions of respect for fundamental freedoms.

4. The Conference takes note of the clauses in the agreement on the cessation of hostilities in Vietnam prohibiting the introduction into Vietnam of foreign troops and military personnel as well as of all kinds of arms and munitions. The Conference also takes note of the declarations made by the Governments of Cambodia and Laos of their resolution not to request foreign aid, whether in war material, in personnel, or in instructors except for the purpose of the effective defense of their territory and, in the case of Laos, to the extent defined by the agreements of the cessation of hostilities in Laos.

5. The Conference takes note of the clauses in the agreement on the cessation of hostilities in Vietnam to the effect that no military base under the control of a foreign State may be established in the regrouping zones of the two parties, the latter having the obligation to see that the zones allotted to them shall not constitute part of any military alliance and shall not be utilized for the resumption of hostilities or in the service of an aggressive policy. The Conference also takes note of the declarations of the Governments of Cambodia and Laos to the effect that they will not join in any agreement with other States if this agreement includes the obligation to participate in a military alliance not in conformity with the principles of the Charter of the United Nations or, in the case of Laos, with the principles of the agreement on the cessation of hostilities in Laos or, so long as their security is not threatened, the obligation to establish bases on Cambodian or Laotian territory for the military forces of foreign powers.

6. The Conference recognizes that the essential purpose of the agreement relating to Vietnam is to settle military questions with a view to ending hostilities and that the military demarcation line is provisional and should not in any way be interpreted as constituting a political or territorial boundary. The Conference expresses its conviction that the execution of the provisions set out in the present declaration and in the agreement on the cessation of hostilities creates the necessary basis for the achievement in the near future of a political settlement in Vietnam.

7. The Conference declares that, so far as Vietnam is concerned, the settlement of political problems, effected on the basis of respect for the principles of independence, unity, and territorial integrity, shall permit the Vietnamese people to enjoy the fundamental freedoms, guaranteed by democratic institutions established as a result of free general elections by secret ballot. In order to ensure that sufficient progress in the restoration of peace has been made, and that all the necessary conditions obtain for free expression of the national will, general elections shall be held in July 1956 under the supervision of an international commission composed of representatives of the Member States of the International Supervisory Commission, referred to in the agreement on the cessation of hostilities. Consultations will be held on this subject between the competent representative authorities of the two zones from July 20, 1955, onward.

8. The provisions of the agreements on the cessation of hostilities intended to ensure the protection of individuals and of property must be most strictly applied and must, in particular, allow everyone in Vietnam to decide freely in which zone he wishes to live.

9. The competent representative authorities of the North and South zones of Vietnam, as well as the authorities of Laos and Cambodia, must not permit any individual or collective reprisals against persons who had collaborated in any way with one of the parties during the war, or against members of such persons' families.

10. The Conference takes note of the declaration of the Government of the French Republic to the effect that it is ready to withdraw its troops from the territory of Cambodia, Laos, and Vietnam, at the request of the Governments concerned and within periods which shall be fixed by agreement between the parties except in the cases where, by agreement between the two parties, a certain number of French troops shall remain at specified points and for a specified time.

11. The Conference takes note of the declaration of the French Government to the effect that for the settlement of all the problems connected with the re-establishment and consolidation of peace in Cambodia, Laos, and Vietnam, the French Government will proceed from the principle of respect for the independence and sovereignty, unity and territorial integrity of Cambodia, Laos, and Vietnam.

12. In their relations with Cambodia, Laos, and Vietnam, each member of the Geneva Conference undertakes to respect the sovereignty, the independence, the unity, and the territorial integrity of the above-mentioned States, and to refrain from any interference in their internal affairs.

13. The members of the Conference agree to consult one another on any question which may be referred to them by the International Supervisory Commission, in order to study such measures as may prove necessary to ensure that the agreements on the cessation of hostilities in Cambodia, Laos, and Vietnam are respected.

*The Pentagon Papers: The Defense Department History of Decisionmaking on Vietnam,*
The Senator Gravel edition, 5 vols, Boston, 1971–72, I, pp. 279–82.

DOCUMENT 9   **THE FOUNDING OF SEATO, SEPTEMBER 1954**

*Press statement by Secretary of State John Foster Dulles, issued upon his arrival at the SEATO organizational meeting in Manila on 6 September 1954.*

We have come here to establish a collective security arrangement for Southeast Asia. In so doing we are acting under the authority, and in accordance with the principles, of the United Nations Charter. What we do is directed against no nation and no peoples. We exercise what the Charter refers to as the inherent right of collective self-defense.

The United States has itself no direct territorial interests in Southeast Asia. Nevertheless, we feel a sense of common destiny with those who have in this area their life and being.

We are united by a common danger, the danger that stems from international communism and its insatiable ambition. We know that wherever it makes gains, as in Indochina, these gains are looked on, not as final solutions, but as bridgeheads for future gains. It is that fact which requires each of us to be concerned with what goes on elsewhere.

The danger manifests itself in many forms. One form is that of open armed aggression.

We can greatly diminish that risk by making clear that an attack upon the treaty area would occasion a reaction so united, so strong and so well-placed that the aggressor would lose more than it could hope to gain.

So our association should bind the members to develop both individual and collective capacity to resist armed attack. The United States is itself seeking to do that and we note with satisfaction the efforts which are being made in this direction in other countries here, such as the Philippines, Thailand and Pakistan. We welcome the historic declaration by the Prime Minister of Australia that Australia was prepared to accept, even in time of peace, overseas military commitments.

It will be necessary to assure that the individual efforts of the various parties to the treaty are used to the best common advantage. Those nations which are represented here cannot match the vast land armies, of which international communism disposes in Asia. For the free nations to attempt to maintain or support formidable land-based forces at every danger point throughout the world would be self-destructive.

Insofar as the United States is concerned, its responsibilities are so vast and so far flung that we believe we serve best by developing the deterrent of mobile striking power, plus strategically placed reserves.

I am confident that through prospective treaty members, by adequate and well-coordinated efforts which are within our capacity, we can establish a power that protects us all.

In addition to the danger of open armed attack there is the danger from subversion and indirect aggression. There is no simple or single formula to cover such risks. To meet them requires dedication, fortitude and resourcefulness, such as was shown here by President Magsaysay.

The opportunities of communism will diminish if trade relationships help the free nations to strengthen their economies. This will require the participation of countries additional to those which are particularly concerned with the security of Southeast Asia. Economic planning, to be adequate, must stimulate trade not only within the Southeast Asia area, but also between that area and South Asia and the West Pacific. Such planning is obviously beyond the scope of this conference. But this conference would not do its duty toward the many who place hope in us if we did not leave here with a well-conceived resolve to unite our efforts with those of others to make the free countries of this area stronger and more vigorous, not only militarily, but also socially and economically.

Some countries, which have a close relationship to the prospective treaty area, are not here. Among these are Cambodia, Laos and Vietnam. Their governments and people can know that we shall have them much in mind, and I hope we shall be able to throw over them some mantle of protection. There are other countries which may subsequently desire to join our defensive grouping. To that end our treaty will, I hope, make provision for the adherence of new members.

There is one aspect of our problem which should always be remembered. That is the yearning of the Asian peoples to be free of 'colonialism.'

International Communism uses 'nationalism' as a slogan for gaining control, and then imposes its own brutal form of imperialism, which is the negation of nationalism.

We are rightly zealous against that Communist threat. But we should be careful lest that zeal lead us inadvertently to offend those who still associate colonialism with the Western powers.

It must be made abundantly clear that we each and all intend to invigorate the independence of the new nations and to promote the processes whereby others become capable of winning and sustaining the independence they desire. Only then can the West and the East work together in true fellowship.

We gather here with some differences to be resolved. That is nothing frightening. Differences are inherent in a society of freedom.

I do not doubt that out of our initial differences we shall develop an area of significant agreement. That is our high duty, both to ourselves and others.

We see that duty dramatically defined as in Northern Vietnam hundreds of thousands are today abandoning their ancient homes to start life anew where they believe they will be free. We are seeing another exodus, such as took millions out of Communist East Germany and millions out of Communist North Korea.

Those of us who are free and strong and not yet instantly imperiled are bound in honor to prove that freedom can protect those who, at immense sacrifice, are faithful to freedom.

Let that be the dedication of our conference.

Department of State, Press Release 492, 6 September 1954.

## DOCUMENT 10    THE NLF PROGRAM, DECEMBER 1960

*Program of the National Front for the Liberation of South Vietnam (NLF), December 1960, rallying opposition to the US-backed Diem regime.*

I. *Overthrow the camouflaged colonial regime of the American imperialists and the dictatorial power of Ngo Dinh Diem, servant of the Americans, and institute a government of national democratic union.*

The present South Vietnamese regime is a camouflaged colonial regime dominated by the Yankees, and the South Vietnamese Government is a servile government, implementing faithfully all the policies of the American imperialists. Therefore, this regime must be overthrown and a government of national and democratic union put in its place composed of representatives of all social classes, of all nationalities, of the various political parties, of all religions; patriotic, eminent citizens must take over for the people the control of economic, political, social, and cultural interests and thus bring about independence, democracy, well-being, peace, neutrality, and efforts toward the peaceful unification of the country.

II. *Institute a largely liberal and democratic regime.*

1. Abolish the present constitution of the dictatorial powers of Ngo Dinh

Diem, servant of the Americans. Elect a new National Assembly through universal suffrage. 2. Implement essential democratic liberties: freedom of opinion, of press, of assembly, of movement, of trade-unionism; freedom of religion without any discrimination; and the right of all patriotic organizations of whatever political tendency to carry on normal activities. 3. Proclaim a general amnesty for all political prisoners and the dissolution of concentration camps of all sorts; abolish fascist law 10/59 and all the other antidemocratic laws; authorize the return to the country of all persons persecuted by the American-Diem regime who are now refugees abroad. 4. Interdict all illegal arrests and detections; prohibit torture; and punish all the Diem bullies who have not repented and who have committed crimes against the people.

III. *Establish an independent and sovereign economy, and improve the living conditions of the people.*

1. Suppress the monopolies imposed by American imperialists and their servants; establish an independent and sovereign economy and finances in accordance with the national interests; confiscate to the profit of the nation the properties of the American imperialists and their servants. 2. Support the national bourgeoisie in the reconstruction and development of crafts and industry; provide active protection for national products through the suppression of production taxes and the limitation or prohibition of imports that the national economy is capable of producing; reduce customs fees on raw materials and machines. 3. Revitalize agriculture; modernize production, fishing, and cattle raising; help the farmers in putting to the plow unused land and in developing production; protect the crops and guarantee their disposal. 4. Encourage and reinforce economic relations between the city and country, the plain and the mountain regions; develop commercial exchanges with foreign countries, regardless of their political regime, on the basis of equality and mutual interests. 5. Institute a just and rational system of taxation; eliminate harassing penalties. 6. Implant the labor code; prohibition of discharges of penalties, of ill-treatment of wage earners; improvement of the living conditions of workers and civil servants; imposition of wage scales and protective measures for young apprentices. 7. Organize social welfare: find work for jobless persons; assume the support and protection of orphans, old people, invalids; come to the help of the victims of the Americans and Diemists; organize help for areas hit by bad crops, fires, or natural calamities. 8. Come to help of displaced persons desiring to return to their native areas and to those who wish to remain permanently in the South; improve their working and living conditions. 9. Prohibit expulsions, spoliation, and compulsory concentration of the population; guarantee job security for the urban and rural working populations.

IV. *Reduce land rent; implement agrarian reform with the aim of providing land to the tillers.*
1. Reduce land rent; guarantee to the farmers the right to till the soil; guarantee the property right of accession to fallow lands to those who have cultivated them; guarantee property rights to those farmers who have already received land. 2. Dissolve 'prosperity zones,' and put an end to recruitment for the camps that are called 'agricultural development centers.' Allow those compatriots who already have been forced into 'prosperity zones' and 'agricultural development centers' to return freely to their own lands. 3. Confiscate the land owned by American imperialists and their servants, and distribute it to poor peasants without any land or with insufficient land; redistribute the communal lands on a just and rational basis. 4. By negotiation and on the basis of fair prices, repurchase for distribution to landless peasants or peasants with insufficient land those surplus lands that the owners of large estates will be made to relinquish if their domain exceeds a certain limit, to be determined in accordance with regional particularities. The farmers who benefit from such land distribution will not be compelled to make any payment or to submit to any other conditions.

V. *Develop a national and democratic culture and education.*
1. Combat all forms of culture and education enslaved to Yankee fashions; develop a culture and education that is national, progressive, and at the service of the Fatherland and people. 2. Liquidate illiteracy; increase the number of schools in the fields of general education as well as in those of technical and professional education, in advanced study as well as in other fields; adopt Vietnamese as the vernacular language; reduce the expenses of education and exempt from payment students who are without means; resume the examination system. 3. Promote science and technology and the national letters and arts; encourage and support the intellectuals and artists so as to permit them to develop their talents in the service of national reconstruction. 4. Watch over public health; develop sports and physical education.

VI. *Create a national army devoted to the defense of the Fatherland and the people.*
1. Establish a national army devoted to the defense of the Fatherland and the people; abolish the system of American military advisers. 2. Abolish the draft system; improve the living conditions of the simple soldiers and guarantee their political rights; put an end to ill-treatment of the military; pay particular attention to the dependents of soldiers without means. 3. Reward officers and soldiers having participated in the struggle against the domination by the Americans and their servants; adopt a policy of clemency toward the former collaborators of the Americans and Diemists guilty of crimes against the people but who have finally repented and are

ready to serve the people. 4. Abolish all foreign military bases established on the territory of Vietnam.

VII. *Guarantee equality between the various minorities and between the two sexes; protect the legitimate interests of foreign citizens established in Vietnam and of Vietnamese citizens residing abroad.*
1. Implement the right autonomy of the national minorities: found autonomous zones in the areas with minority population, those zones to be an integral part of the Vietnamese nation. Guarantee equality between the various nationalities: each nationality has the right to use and develop its language and writing system, to maintain or to modify freely its *mores* and customs; abolish the policy of the Americans and Diemists of racial discrimination and forced assimilation. Create conditions permitting the national minorities to reach the general level of progress of the population: development of their economy and culture; formation of cadres of minority nationalities. 2. Establish equality between the two sexes; women shall have equal rights with men from all viewpoints (political, economic, cultural, social, etc.). 3. Protect the legitimate interests of foreign citizens established in Vietnam. 4. Defend and take care of the interests of Vietnamese citizens residing abroad.

VIII. *Promote a foreign policy of peace and neutrality.*
1. Cancel all unequal treaties that infringe upon the sovereignty of the people and that were concluded with other countries by the servants of the Americans. 2. Establish diplomatic relations with all countries, regardless of their political regime, in accordance with the principles of peaceful coexistence adopted at the Bandung Conference. 3. Develop close solidarity with peace-loving nations and neutral countries; develop free relations with the nations of Southeast Asia, in particular with Cambodia and Laos. 4. Stay out of any military bloc; refuse any military alliance with another country. 5. Accept economic aid from any country willing to help us without attaching any conditions to such help.

IX. *Re-establish normal relations between the two zones, and prepare for the peaceful reunification of the country.*
The peaceful reunification of the country constitutes the dearest desire of all our compatriots throughout the country. The National Liberation Front of South Vietnam advocates the peaceful reunification by stages on the basis of negotiations and through the seeking of ways and means in conformity with the interests of the Vietnamese nation. While awaiting this reunification, the governments of the two zones will, on the basis of negotiations, promise to banish all separatist and war-mongering propaganda and not to use force to settle differences between the zones. Commercial and cultural exchanges be-

tween the two zones will be implemented; the inhabitants of the two zones will be free to move about throughout the country as their family and business interests indicate. The freedom of postal exchanges will be guaranteed.

X. *Struggle against all aggressive war; actively defend universal peace.*
1. Struggle against all aggressive war and against all forms of imperialist domination; support the national emancipation movements of the various peoples. 2. Banish all war-mongering propaganda; demand general disarmament and the prohibition of nuclear weapons; and advocate the utilization of atomic energy for peaceful purposes. 3. Support all movements of struggle for peace, democracy, and social progress throughout the world; contribute actively to the defense of peace in South-east Asia and in the world.

Marvin E. Gettleman et al., eds, Vietnam and America: The Most Comprehensive<br>Documentary History of the Vietnam War, 2nd edn, New York: Grove Press, 1995,<br>pp. 188–91.

### DOCUMENT 11    THE CRISIS IN LAOS, JANUARY 1961

*President Eisenhower briefs John F. Kennedy on the crisis in Laos, 19 January 1961.*

President Eisenhower opened the session on Laos by stating that the United States was determined to preserve the independence of Laos. It was his opinion that if Laos should fall to the Communists, then it would be just a question of time until South Vietnam, Cambodia, Thailand, and Burma would collapse. He felt that the Communists had designs on all of South-east Asia, and that it would be a tragedy to permit Laos to fall.

President Eisenhower gave a brief review of the various moves and coups that had taken place in Laos involving the Pathet Lao, Souvanna Phouma, Boun Oum, and Kong Le. He said that the evidence was clear that Communist China and North Vietnam were determined to destroy the independence of Laos. He also added that the Russians were sending in substantial supplies in support of the Pathet Lao in an effort to overturn the government. ...

President Eisenhower said with considerable emotion that Laos was the key to the entire area of Southeast Asia. He said that if we permitted Laos to fall, then we would have to write off all the area. He stated that we must not permit a Communist take-over. He reiterated that we should make every effort to persuade member nations of SEATO or the ICC to accept the burden with us to defend the freedom of Laos.

As he concluded these remarks, President Eisenhower stated it was imperative that Laos be defended. He said that the United States should accept this task with our allies, if we could persuade them, and alone if we could not. He added that 'our unilateral intervention would be our last desperate hope' in the event we were unable to prevail upon the other signatories to join us. ...

Commenting upon President Eisenhower's statement that we would have to go to the support of Laos alone if we could not persuade others to proceed with us, President-elect Kennedy asked the question as to how long it would take to put an American division into Laos. Secretary Gates replied that it would take from twelve to seventeen days but that some of that time could be saved if American forces, then in the Pacific, could be utilized. Secretary Gates added that the American forces were in excellent shape and that modernization of the Army was making good progress.

President-elect Kennedy commented upon the seriousness of the situation in Laos and in Southeast Asia and asked if the situation seemed to be approaching a climax. General Eisenhower stated that the entire proceeding was extremely confused but that it was clear that this country was obligated to support the existing government in Laos. ...

> *The Pentagon Papers: the Defense Department History of Decisionmaking on Vietnam,*
> The Senator Gravel edition, 5 vols, Boston, 1971–72, II, pp. 635–7.

## DOCUMENT 12   THE TAYLOR REPORT, NOVEMBER 1961

*Cable by General Maxwell Taylor, Kennedy's military adviser, to the president, 1 November 1961, in which Taylor recommends the dispatch of US military force into South Vietnam.*

This message is for the purpose of presenting my reasons for recommending the introduction of a U.S. military force into SVN [South Vietnam]. I have reached the conclusion that this is an essential action if we are to reverse the present downward trend of events in spite of a full recognition of the following disadvantages:

a. The strategic reserve of U.S. forces is presently so weak that we can ill afford any detachment of forces to a peripheral area of the Communist bloc where they will be pinned down for an uncertain duration.

b. Although U.S. prestige is already engaged in SVN, it will become more so by the sending of troops.

c. If the first contingent is not enough to accomplish the necessary results, it will be difficult to resist the pressure to reinforce. If the ultimate result sought is the closing of the frontiers and the clean-up of the insurgents within SVN, there is no limit to our possible commitment (unless we attack the source in Hanoi).

d. The introduction of U.S. forces may increase tensions and risk escalation into a major war in Asia.

On the other side of the argument, there can be no action so convincing of U.S. seriousness of purpose and hence so reassuring to the people and Government of SVN and to our other friends and allies in SEA [Southeast Asia] as the introduction of U.S. forces into SVN. The views of indigenous and U.S. officials consulted on our trip were unanimous on this point. I have just seen Saigon [cable] 575 to State and suggest that it be read in connection with this message.

The size of the U.S. force introduced need not be great to provide the military presence necessary to produce the desired effect on national morale in SVN and on international opinion. A bare token, however, will not suffice; it must have a significant value. The kinds of tasks which it might undertake which would have a significant value are suggested in Baguio [cable] 0005. They are:

a. Provide a U.S. military presence capable of raising national morale and of showing to SEA the seriousness of the U.S. intent to resist a Communist takeover.

b. Conduct logistical operations in support of military and flood relief operations.

c. Conduct such combat operations as are necessary for self-defense and for the security of the area in which they are stationed.

d. Provide an emergency reserve to back up the Armed Forces of the GVN in the case of a heightened military crisis.

e. Act as an advance party of such additional forces as may be introduced if CINCPAC [U.S. Commander in Chief, Pacific] or SEATO contingency plans are invoked.

It is noteworthy that this force is not proposed to clear the jungles and forests of VC [Vietcong] guerrillas. That should be the primary task of the Armed Forces of Vietnam for which they should be specifically organized, trained and stiffened with ample U.S. advisors down to combat battalion levels. However, the U.S. troops may be called upon to engage in combat to protect themselves, their working parties, and the area in which they live. As a general reserve, they might be thrown into action (with U.S. agreement) against large, formed guerrilla bands which have abandoned the forests for attacks on major targets. But in general, our forces should not engage in small-scale guerrilla operations in the jungle.

As an area for the operations of U.S. troops, SVN is not an excessively difficult or unpleasant place to operate. While the border areas are rugged and heavily forested, the terrain is comparable to parts of Korea where U.S. troops learned to live and work without too much effort. However, these border areas, for reasons stated above, are not the places to engage our forces. In the High Plateau and in the coastal plain where U.S. troops would probably be stationed, these jungle-forest conditions do not exist to any great extent. The most unpleasant feature in the coastal areas would be the heat and, in the Delta, the mud left behind by the flood. The High Plateau offers no particular obstacle to the stationing of U.S. troops.

The extent to which the Task Force would engage in flood relief activities in the Delta will depend upon further study of the problem there. As reported in Saigon 537, I see considerable advantages in playing up this aspect of the TF [Task Force] mission. I am presently inclined to favor a dual mission, initially help to the flood area and subsequently use in any other area of SVN where its resources can be used effectively to give tangible support in the struggle against the VC. However, the possibility of emphasizing the humanitarian mission will wane if we wait long in moving in our forces or in linking our stated purpose with the emergency conditions created by the flood.

The risks of backing into a major Asian war by way of SVN are present but are not impressive. NVN [North Vietnam] is extremely vulnerable to conventional bombing, a weakness which should be exploited diplomatically in convincing Hanoi to lay off SVN. Both the D.R.V. and the Chicoms [Chinese communists] would face severe logistical difficulties in trying to maintain strong forces in the field in SEA, difficulties which we share but by no means to the same degree. There is no case for fearing a mass onslaught of Communist manpower into SVN and its neighboring states, particularly if our airpower is allowed a free hand against logistical targets. Finally, the starvation conditions in China should discourage Communist leaders there from being militarily venturesome for some time to come.

By the foregoing line of reasoning, I have reached the conclusion that the introduction of [word illegible] military Task Force without delay offers definitely more advantage that it creates risks and difficulties. In fact, I do not believe that our program to save SVN will succeed without it. If the concept is approved, the exact size and composition of the force should be determined by Sec Def in consultation with the JCS, the Chief MAAG [Military Assistance Advisory Group] and CINCPAC. My own feeling is that the initial size should not exceed about 8000, of which a preponderant number would be in logistical-type units. After acquiring experience in operating in SVN, this initial force will require reorganization and adjustment to the local scene.

As CINCPAC will point out, any forces committed to SVN will need to be replaced by additional forces to his area from the stategic reserve in the U.S. Also, any troops to SVN are in addition to those which may be required to execute SEATO Plan 5 in Laos. Both facts should be taken into account in current considerations of the FY [fiscal year] 1963 budget which bear upon the permanent increase which should be made in the U.S. military establishment to maintain our strategic position for the long pull.

Kennedy Library, box 301, National Security Files, Vietnam Country Series, Memos and Miscellaneous, Confidential, 1 November 1961, Boston, MA.

## DOCUMENT 13    US SUPPORT FOR THE OVERTHROW OF DIEM, AUGUST 1963

*Cable from Henry Cabot Lodge, the newly arrived US ambassador to South Vietnam, to Secretary of State Dean Rusk, 29 August 1963.*

1. We are launched on a course from which there is no respectable turning back: the overthrow of the Diem government. There is no turning back in part because U.S. prestige is already publicly committed to this end in large measure and will become more so as the facts leak out. In a more fundamental sense, there is no turning back because there is no possibility, in my view, that the war can be won under a Diem administration, still less that Diem or any member of the family can govern the country in a way to gain the support of the people who count, i.e., the educated class in and out of government service, civil and military – not to mention the American people. In the last few months (and especially days) they have in fact positively alienated these people to an incalculable degree. So that I am personally in full agreement with the policy which I was instructed to carry out by last Sunday's telegram.

2. The chance of bringing off a Generals' coup depends on them to some extent; but it depends at least as much on us.

3. We should proceed to make all-out effort to get Generals to move promptly. To do so we should have authority to do following:

(a) That Gen. Harkins repeat to Generals personally message previously transmitted by CAS [Covert Action branch, Saigon Office of the CIA] officers. This should establish their authenticity. Gen. Harkins should have order on this.

(b) If nevertheless Generals insist on public statement that U.S. aid to VN through Diem regime has been stopped, we would agree, on express understanding that Generals will have started at same time. (We would seek persuade Generals that it would be better to hold this card for use in event of stalemate. We hope it will not be necessary to do this at all.)

(c) VNese Generals doubt that we have the will power, courage, and determination to see this thing through. They are haunted by the idea that we will run out on them even though we have told them pursuant to instructions, that the game had started.

[Point 4 not published]

5. We must press on for many reasons. Some of these are:

(a) Explosiveness of the present situation which may well lead to riots and violence if issue of discontent with regime is not met. Out of this could come a pro-Communist or at best a neutralist set of politicians.

(b) The fact that war cannot be won with the present regime.

(c) Our own reputation for steadfastness and our willingness to stultify ourselves.

(d) If proposed action is suspended, I believe a body blow will be dealt to respect for us by VNese Generals. Also, all those who expect U.S. to straighten out this situation will feel let down. Our help to the regime in past years inescapably gives a responsibility which we cannot avoid.

6. I realize that this course involves a very substantial risk of losing VN. It also involves some additional risk to American lives. I would never propose it if I felt there was a reasonable chance of holding VN with Diem.

[Point 7 unavailable.]

8. ... Gen. Harkins thinks I should ask Diem to get rid of the Nhus before starting the Generals' action. But I believe that such a step has no chance of getting the desired result and would have the very serious effect of being regarded by the Generals as a sign of American indecision and delay. I believe this is a risk which we should not run. The Generals distrust us too much already. Another point is that Diem would certainly ask for time to consider such a far-reaching request. This would give the ball to Nhu. ...

Marvin E. Gettleman et al., eds, *Vietnam and America: The Most Comprehensive Documentary History of the Vietnam War*, 2nd edn, New York: Grove Press, 1995, pp. 227–8.

## DOCUMENT 14  THE KENNEDY ADMINISTRATION DISCOURAGES PRESS CALLS FOR NEGOTIATIONS, NOVEMBER 1963

*Memorandum from Michael V. Forrestal of the National Security Council staff to National Security Adviser McGeorge Bundy, 13 November 1963.*

Washington, November 13, 1963.

I had a brief talk with Bob Kleiman of the *New York Times* editorial board this morning. I told him that I thought the Halberstam article in this morning's edition was irresponsible and mostly reflected a personal animus against General Harkins instead of accurate news reporting. Kleiman admitted that this might be so, but pointed out that there must have been some differences of opinion between the Embassy and MACV, since Halberstam quoted inconsistent Embassy sources and MACV public statements.

Kleiman suggested rather strongly that we move as soon as possible toward a reconvening of the Geneva Conference and a negotiated settlement of the differences between North and South Vietnam. He argued that the political strength of the South will never be as strong again as it will be during the next few months, and that we should seize this opportunity for negotiations before the situation deteriorated and we found ourselves back in a 10-year, Malayan-type effort. In connection with such negotiations he raised the possibility of effecting a mass population transfer in an effort to get all of the Viet Cong moved from the South back up to the North.

I told him that I had great difficulty with this suggestion and thought that it would be folly to pursue this line at the present time. South Vietnam was still not strong enough to approach the bargaining table with any hope of coming away whole. Furthermore, there was no indication that responsible Vietnamese *in Vietnam* would view the prospects of a new Geneva Conference as anything less than a complete sellout by the U.S. I emphasized that we definitely looked toward the time when South Vietnam would be strong enough to deal with the North on at least a basis of equality. I referred to the President's statement of last year and the NSC statement of last month, indicating that the U.S. was prepared to withdraw its presence from South Vietnam as soon as Hanoi ceased its interference in the South or as soon as the South was able to handle the problem on its own. We had not yet reached that point, however. I also questioned whether a population transfer would be feasible in view of the difficulty of identifying the bulk of the Viet Cong, to say nothing of the political problems involved in a forced emigration.

Kleiman will no doubt continue to peddle his Geneva Conference idea, and we should be preparing ourselves to counter it.

Kennedy Library, box 202, National Security Files, Vietnam Country Series, Memos and Miscellaneous, Confidential, 13 November 1963, Boston, MA.

## DOCUMENT 15    THE McNAMARA REPORT, DECEMBER 1963

*Secretary of Defense Robert McNamara to President Johnson, 21 December 1963, reporting on problems identified during a two-day visit to South Vietnam.*

In accordance with your request this morning, this is a summary of my conclusions after my visit to Vietnam on December 19–20.

1. *Summary* The situation is very disturbing. Current trends, unless reversed in the next 2–3 months, will lead to neutralization at best and more likely to a Communist-controlled state.

2. *The new government* is the greatest source of concern. It is indecisive and drifting. Although Minh states that he, rather than the Committee of Generals, is making decisions, it is not clear that this is actually so. In any event, neither he nor the Committee are experienced in political administration and so far they show little talent for it. There is no clear concept on how to re-shape or conduct the strategic hamlet program; the Province

Chiefs, most of whom are new and inexperienced, are receiving little or no direction because the generals are so preoccupied with essentially political affairs. A specific example of the present situation is that General [name illegible] is spending little or no time commanding III Corps, which is in the vital zone around Saigon and needs full-time direction. I made these points as strongly as possible to Minh, Don, Kim, and Tho.

3. *The Country Team* is the second major weakness. It lacks leadership, has been poorly informed, and is not working to a common plan. A recent example of confusion had been conflicting USOM [United States Operations Mission] and military recommendations both to the Government of Vietnam and to Washington on the size of the military budget. Above all, Lodge has virtually no official contact with Harkins. Lodge sends in reports with major military implications without showing them to Harkins, and does not show Harkins important incoming traffic. My impression is that Lodge simply does not know how to conduct a coordinated administration. This has of course been stressed to him both by Dean Rusk and myself (and also by John McCone), and I do not think he is consciously rejecting our advice; he has just operated as a loner all his life and cannot readily change now. ...

4. *Viet Cong progress* has been great during the period since the coup, with my best guess being that the situation has in fact been deteriorating in the countryside since July to a far greater extent than we realized because of our undue dependence on distorted Vietnamese reporting. The Viet Cong now control very high proportions of the people in certain key provinces, particularly those directly south and west of Saigon. The Strategic Hamlet Program was seriously over-extended in those provinces, and the Viet Cong has been able to destroy many hamlets, while others have been abandoned or in some cases betrayed or pillaged by the government's own Self-Defense Corps. In these key provinces, the Viet Cong have destroyed almost all major roads, and are collecting taxes at will.

As remedial measures, we must get the government to reallocate its military forces so that its effective strength in these provinces is essentially doubled. We also need to have major increases in both military and USOM staffs, to sizes that will give us a reliable, independent U.S. appraisal of the status of operations. Thirdly, realistic pacification plans must be prepared, allocating adequate time to secure the remaining government-controlled areas and work out from there.

This gloomy picture prevails predominantly in the provinces around the capital and in the Delta action to accomplish each of these objectives was started while we were in Saigon. The situation in the northern and central areas is considerably better, and does not seem to have deteriorated substantially in recent months. General Harkins still hopes these areas may be made reasonably secure by the latter half of next year. ...

5. *Infiltration* of men and equipment from North Vietnam continues using (a) land corridors through Laos and Cambodia; (b) the Mekong River waterways from Cambodia; (c) some possible entry from the sea and the tip of the Delta. The best guess is that 1000–1500 Viet Cong cadres entered South Vietnam from Laos in the first nine months of 1963. The Mekong route (and also the possible sea entry) is apparently used for heavier weapons and ammunition and raw materials which have been turning up in increasing numbers in the south and of which we have captured a few shipments. ...

6. *Plans for Covert Action into North Vietnam* were prepared as we had requested and were an excellent job. They present a wide variety of sabotage and psychological operations against North Vietnam from which I believe we should aim to select those that provide maximum pressure with minimum risk. In accordance with your direction at the meeting, General Krulak of the JCS is chairing a group that will lay out a program in the next ten days for your consideration. ...

Neil Sheehan et al., eds, *The Pentagon Papers as Published by the New York Times,* New York: Quadrangle Books, 1971, pp. 271–4.

## DOCUMENT 16   THE GULF OF TONKIN RESOLUTION, AUGUST 1964

*On 7 August 1964, Congress – by a vote of 416–0 in the House and 88–2 in the Senate – handed President Johnson the Gulf of Tonkin resolution, the closest approximation to a declaration of war passed during all the years of US combat in Vietnam.*

Whereas naval units of the Communist regime in Vietnam, in violation of the principles of the Charter of the United Nations and of international law, have deliberately and repeatedly attacked United States naval vessels lawfully present in international waters, and have thereby created a serious threat to international peace; and

Whereas these attacks are part of a deliberate and systematic campaign of aggression that the Communist regime in North Vietnam has been waging against its neighbors and the nations joined with them in the collective defense of their freedom; and

Whereas the United States is assisting the peoples of southeast Asia to protect their freedom and has no territorial, military or political ambitions in that area, but desires only that these peoples should be left in peace to work out their own destinies in their own way: Now, therefore, be it Resolved by the Senate and House of Representatives of the United States of America in Congress assembled, That the Congress approves and supports the determination of the President, as Commander in Chief, to take all necessary measures to repel any armed attack against the forces of the United States and to prevent further aggression.

SEC. 2. The United States regards as vital to its national interest and to world peace the maintenance of international peace and security in south-east Asia. Consonant with the Constitution of the United States and the charter of the United Nations and in accordance with its obligations under the South-east Asia Collective Defense Treaty, the United States is, therefore, prepared, as the President determines, to take all necessary steps, including the use of armed force, to assist any member or protocol state of the Southeast Asia Collective Defense Treaty requesting assistance in defense of its freedom.

SEC. 3 This resolution shall expire when the President shall determine that the peace and security of the area is reasonably assured by international conditions created by action of the United Nations or otherwise, except that it may be terminated earlier by concurrent resolution of the Congress.

*US Department of State Bulletin* 51, 1313 (24 August 1964), p. 268.

## DOCUMENT 17   DELIBERATING ESCALATION, DECEMBER 1964

*Telegram from Lyndon Johnson to Maxwell Taylor, the US ambassador in Saigon, 30 December 1964.*

Washington, December 30, 1964 – 11.15 a.m.

CAP 64375. For Amb Taylor only at opening of business day from the President of the United States.

1. I talked at length with Dean Rusk and Mac Bundy about your recommendation of reprisal for the Brink bombing. While I fully recognize the force of your feeling, which was strongly supported by a number of good men here, I myself concurred with Dean Rusk and Bob McNamara, who for overlapping reasons felt that we should not now make an air reprisal in North Vietnam. In reaching this decision, we were guided by a number of considerations peculiar to this episode. First and foremost, of course, is the continuing political turmoil in Saigon. If we ourselves were uncertain for several days about the source of the Brink's bombing, we cannot expect the world to be less uncertain. I know that 'the Liberation Front' has claimed the credit, but we all know that radio claims are not the most persuasive evidence of what has actually happened. This uncertainty is just one sign of the general confusion in South Vietnam which makes me feel strongly that we are not now in a position which justifies a policy of immediate reprisal.

2. What I want to do in this message is to share my own thinking with you and to ask for your full comment so that we can lay a basis of under-

standing that will give us a base-line not only for prompt reprisals but for other actions, mainly within South Vietnam, which can help to turn the tide.

3. I continue to feel very strongly that we ought not to be widening the battle until we get our dependents out of South Vietnam. I know that you have not agreed with this view in the past, and I recognize that there are some agencies which may face recruiting difficulties if dependents are removed, but no argument I have yet heard overrides the fact that we are facing a war in Saigon and we are considering actions which may bring strong communist reaction, if not by air, at least by a concentrated VC [Vietcong] effort against Americans; this last is estimated by intelligence community as the very likely enemy reaction to a reprisal like air attack on target 36. In this situation I simply do not understand why it is helpful to have women and children in the battle zone, and my own readiness to authorize larger actions will be very much greater if we can remove the dependents and get ourselves into real fighting trim. Neither this nor any other part of this message is intended as an order, but I do wish you to understand the strength of my feeling and the fact that I have not been persuaded by arguments I have heard on the other side.

4. I also have real doubts about ordering reprisals in cases in which our own security seems, at first glance, to have been very weak. I notice in your last talk with Huong that he seems to have the same worry. I do not want to be drawn into a large-scale military action against North Vietnam simply because our own people are careless or imprudent. This too may be an unfair way of stating the matter, but I have not yet been told in any convincing way why aircraft cannot be protected from mortar attacks and officers quarters from large bombs.

5. I am still worried, too, by our lack of progress in communicating sensitively and persuasively with the various groups in South Vietnam. I recognize the very great problems which we face in dealing with groups which are immature and often irresponsible. But I still do not feel that we are making the all-out effort of political persuasion which is called for.

In particular, I wonder whether we are making full use of the kind of Americans who have shown a knack for this kind of communication in the past. I do not want to pick out any particular individual because I do not know these men at first hand. But I do think that we ought to be ready to make full use of the specialized skills of men who are skillful with Vietnamese, even if they are not always the easiest men to handle in a country team. In this, again, I recognize that you must have the final responsibility for the selection and management of your country team, and I am giving no order but only raising a question which is increasingly insistent in my own mind.

To put it another way, I continue to believe that we should have the most sensitive, persistent, and attentive Americans that we can find in touch with

Vietnamese of every kind and quality, and reinforced by Englishmen, and Buddhists, and labor leaders and agricultural experts, and other free men of every kind and type, who may have skills to contribute in a contest on all fronts. I just do not think we should leave any stone unturned, and I do not have the feeling that we have yet done everything that we can in these areas.

6. Every time I get a military recommendation it seems to me that it calls for large-scale bombing. I have never felt that this war will be won from the air, and it seems to me that what is much more needed and would be more effective is a larger and stronger use of Rangers and Special Forces and Marines, or other appropriate military strength on the ground and on the scene. I am ready to look with great favor on that kind of increased American effort, directed at the guerrillas and aimed to stiffen the aggressiveness of Vietnamese military units up and down the line. Any recommendation that you or General Westmoreland make in this sense will have immediate attention from me, although I know that it may involve the acceptance of larger American sacrifice. We have been building our strength to fight this kind of war ever since 1961, and I myself am ready to substantially increase the number of Americans in Vietnam if it is necessary to provide this kind of fighting force against the Viet Cong.

7. I am not saying that all this has to be done before there can be any reprisals. Indeed, as I say, I am not giving any orders at all in this message. But I am inclined to offer this suggestion:

I would like to see you move more strongly in four directions:

(1) The removal of dependents.
(2) The stiffening of our own security arrangements to protect our own people and forces.
(3) A much wider and more varied attempt to get good political relations with all Vietnamese groups.
(4) An intensified US stiffening on-the-ground by Rangers and Special Forces or other appropriate elements.

If you can give me either progress or persuasive arguments on these matters, I would look with favor on the execution of immediate and automatic reprisal against targets like No. 36 in the event of further attacks. I myself believe that such reprisals should have a Vietnamese component whenever possible, but I hope that the necessary consultation for such a component can be kept down to a very few hours so that we could react with a speed which will show beyond any question what caused our action.

8. Let me repeat once more that this whole message is intended to show you the state of my thinking and to ask for your frankest comments and responses. I know that you are the man on the spot and I know what a very

heavy load you are carrying. I am grateful for it and I want you to know in turn that you have my complete confidence in the biggest and hardest job that we have overseas. But in this tough situation in which the final responsibility is mine and the stakes are very high indeed, I have wanted you to have this full and frank statement of the way I see it.

US Department of State, *Foreign Relations of the United States, 1964–1968 – Vietnam*, Washington, DC: Government Printing Office, 1993, I, pp. 1057–9.

### DOCUMENT 18   HUMPHREY ADVISES AGAINST ESCALATION, FEBRUARY 1965

*Memorandum from Vice President Hubert H. Humphrey to Johnson, 17 February 1965, in which Humphrey warns against Americanizing the war.*

Washington, February 17, 1965.

SUBJECT Vietnam

I would like to share with you my views on the political consequences of certain courses of action that have been proposed in regard to U.S. policy in Southeast Asia. I refer both to the domestic political consequences here in the United States and to the international political consequences.

*A. Domestic Political Consequences.*
  1. *1964 Campaign.*
  Although the question of U.S. involvement in Vietnam is and should be a non-partisan question, there have always been significant differences in approach to the Asian question between the Republican Party and the Democratic Party. These came out in the 1964 campaign. The Republicans represented both by Goldwater, and the top Republican leaders in Congress, favored a quick, total military solution in Vietnam, to be achieved through military escalation of the war.

  The Democratic position emphasized the complexity of a Vietnam situation involving both political, social and military factors; the necessity of staying in Vietnam as long as necessary; recognition that the war will be won or lost chiefly in South Vietnam.

  In Vietnam, as in Korea, the Republicans have attacked the Democrats either for failure to use our military power to 'win' a total victory, or alternatively for losing the country to the Communists. The Democratic position has always been one of firmness in the face of Communist pressure but restraint in the use of military force; it has sought to obtain the best possible settlement without provoking a nuclear World War III; it has sought to leave open face-saving options to an opponent when necessary to avoid a nuclear show-down. When grave risks have been necessary, as in the case of Cuba, they have been taken. But here again a face-saving option was permitted the opponent. In all instances the Democratic position has included a balancing of both political and military factors.

Today the Administration is being charged by some of its critics with adopting the Goldwater position on Vietnam. While this is *not* true of the Administration's position as defined by the President, it is true that many key advisors in the Government are advocating a policy markedly similar to the Republican policy as defined by Goldwater.

2. *Consequences for other policies advocated by a Democratic Administration.*

The Johnson Administration is associated both at home and abroad with a policy of progress toward détente with the Soviet bloc, a policy of limited arms control, and a policy of new initiatives for peace. A full-scale military attack on North Vietnam – with the attendant risk of an open military clash with Communist China – would risk gravely undermining other U.S. policies. It would eliminate for the time being any possible exchange between the President and Soviet leaders; it would postpone any progress on arms control; it would encourage the Soviet Union and China to end their rift; it would seriously hamper our efforts to strengthen relations with our European allies; it would weaken our position in the United Nations; it might require a call-up of reservists if we were to get involved in a large-scale land war – and a consequent increase in defense expenditures; it would tend to shift the Administration's emphasis from its Great Society oriented programs to further military outlays; finally and most important it would damage the image of the President of the United States – and that of the United States itself.

3. *Involvement in a full scale war with North Vietnam would not make sense to the majority of the American people.*

American wars have to be politically understandable by the American public. There has to be a cogent, convincing case if we are to have sustained public support. In World Wars I and II we had this. In Korea we were moving under UN auspices to defend South Korea against dramatic, across-the-border conventional aggression. Yet even with those advantages, we could not sustain American political support for fighting the Chinese in Korea in 1952.

Today in Vietnam we lack the very advantages we had in Korea. The public is worried and confused. Our rationale for action has shifted away now even from the notion that we are there as advisors on request of a free government – to the simple argument of our 'national interest.' We have not succeeded in making this 'national interest' interesting enough at home or abroad to generate support.

4. From a political viewpoint, the American people find it hard to understand why we risk World War III by enlarging a war under terms we found unacceptable 12 years ago in Korea, particularly since the chances of success are slimmer.

Politically, people think of North Vietnam and North Korea. They recall all the 'lessons' of 1950–53:

a. The limitations of air power.

b. The Chinese intervention.

c. The 'never again club' – never again GI's fighting a land war against Asians in Asia.

d. The Eisenhower Administration's compromise which represented a frank recognition of all these factors.

If a war with China was ruled out by the Truman and Eisenhower Administrations alike in 1952–3, at a time when we alone had nuclear weapons, people find it hard to contemplate such a war with China now. No one really believes the Soviet Union would allow us to destroy Communist China with nuclear weapons, as Russia's status as a world power would be undermined if she did.

5. *Absence of confidence in the Government of South Vietnam.*

Politically, people can't understand why we would run grave risks to support a country which is totally unable to put its own house in order. The chronic instability in Saigon directly undermines American political support for our policy.

6. Politically, it is hard to justify over a long period of time sustained, large-scale U.S. air bombardments across a border as a response to camouflaged, often non-sensational, elusive, small-scale terror which has been going on for 10 years in what looks like a civil war in the South.

7. Politically, in Washington and across the country, the opposition is more Democratic than Republican.

8. Politically, it is always hard to cut losses. But the Johnson Administration is in a stronger position to do so than any Administration in this century. 1965 is the year of minimum political risk for the Johnson Administration. Indeed it is the first year when we can face the Vietnam problem without being preoccupied with the political repercussions from the Republican right. As indicated earlier, the political problems are likely to come from new and different sources if we pursue an enlarged military policy very long (Democratic liberals, Independents, Labor, Church groups).

9. Politically, we now risk creating the impression that we are the prisoner of events in Vietnam. This blurs the Administration's leadership role and has spill-over effects across the board. It also helps erode confidence and credibility in our policies.

10. The President is personally identified with, and admired for, political ingenuity. He will be expected to put all his great political sense to work now for international political solutions. People will be counting upon him to use on the world scene his unrivalled talents as a political leader.

They will be watching to see how he makes this transition. The best possible outcome a year from now would be a Vietnam settlement which turns out to be better than was in the cards because the President's political talents for the first time came to grips with a fateful world crisis and so successfully. It goes without saying that the subsequent domestic political benefits of such an outcome, and such a new dimension for the President, would be enormous.

11. If on the other hand, we find ourselves leading from frustration to escalation, and end up short of a war with China but embroiled deeper in fighting with Vietnam over the next few months, political opposition will steadily mount. It will underwrite all the negativism and disillusionment which we already have about foreign involvement generally – with direct spill-over effects politically for all the Democratic internationalist programs to which we are committed – AID, UN, disarmament, and activist world policies generally.

## B. *International Political Implications of Vietnam*

1. What is our goal, our ultimate objective in Vietnam? Is our goal to restore a military balance between North and South Vietnam so as to go to the conference table later to negotiate a settlement? I believe it is the latter. If so, what is the optimum time for achieving the most favorable combination of factors to achieve this goal?

If ultimately a negotiated settlement is our aim, when do we start developing a *political track, in addition to the military one,* that might lead us to the conference table? I believe we should develop the political track earlier rather than later. We should take the initiative on the political side and not end up being dragged to a conference as an unwilling participant. This does not mean we should cease all programs of military pressure. But we should distinguish carefully between those military actions necessary to reach our political goal of a negotiated settlement, and those likely to provoke open Chinese military intervention.

We should not underestimate the likelihood of Chinese intervention and repeat the mistake of the Korean War. If we begin to bomb further north in Vietnam, the likelihood is great of an encounter with the Chinese Air Force operating from sanctuary bases across the border. Once the Chinese Air Force is involved, Peking's full prestige will be involved as she cannot afford to permit her Air Force to be destroyed. To do so would undermine, if not end, her role as a great power in Asia.

Confrontation with the Chinese Air Force can easily lead to massive retaliation by the Chinese in South Vietnam. What is our response to this? Do we bomb Chinese air bases and nuclear installations? If so, will not the Soviet Union honor its treaty of friendship and come to China's assistance? I believe there is a good chance that it would – thereby involving us in a war with both China and the Soviet Union. Here again, we must remember the consequences for the Soviet Union of *not* intervening if China's military power is destroyed by the U.S.

US Department of State, *Foreign Relations of the United States, 1964–1968 – Vietnam*, Washington, DC: Government Printing Office, 1995, II, pp. 309–13.

## DOCUMENT 19    THE JOHNS HOPKINS SPEECH, APRIL 1965

*President Johnson justifies US involvement in Vietnam in a speech at Johns Hopkins University in Baltimore, 7 April 1965.*

Viet-Nam is far away from this quiet campus. We have no territory there, nor do we seek any. The war is dirty and brutal and difficult. ...

Why must we take this painful road? ...

We fight because we must fight if we are to live in a world where every country can shape its own destiny. And only in such a world will our own freedom be finally secure. ...

The first reality is that North Viet-Nam has attacked the independent nation of South Viet-Nam. Its object is total conquest.

Of course, some of the people of South Viet-Nam are participating in attack on their own government. But trained men and supplies, orders and arms, flow in a constant stream from north to south. ...

Over this war – and all Asia – is another reality: the deepening shadow of Communist China. The rulers in Hanoi are urged on by Peking. ...

Why are these realities our concern? Why are we in south Viet-Nam?

*We are there because we have a promise to keep.* Since 1954 every American president has offered support to the people of South Viet-Nam. We have helped to build, and we have helped to defend. Thus, over many years, we have made a national pledge to help South Viet-Nam defend its independence.

And I intend to keep that promise. ...

*We are also there to strengthen world order.* Around the globe, from Berlin to Thailand, are people whose well-being rests, in part, on the belief that they can count on us if they are attacked. To leave Viet-Nam to its fate would shake the confidence of all these people in the value of an American commitment and in the value of America's word. The result would be increased unrest and instability, and even wider war.

*We are also there because there are great stakes in the balance.* Let no one think for a moment that retreat from Viet-Nam would bring an end to the conflict. The battle would be renewed in one country and then another. The central lesson of our time is that the appetite of aggression is never satisfied. To withdraw from one battlefield means only to prepare for the next. We must say in southeast Asia – as we did in Europe – in the words of the Bible: 'Hitherto shalt thou come, but no further.' ...

Our objective is the independence of South Viet-Nam, and its freedom from attack. We want nothing for ourselves – only that the people of South Viet-Nam be allowed to guide their own country in their own way.

We will do everything necessary to reach that objective. And we will do only what is absolutely necessary.

In recent months attacks on South Viet-Nam were stepped up. Thus, it became necessary for us to increase our response and to make attacks by air. This is not a change of purpose. It is a change in what we believe that purpose requires. ...

... [[P]eace demands an independent South Viet-Nam – securely guaranteed and able to shape its own relationships to all others – free from outside interference – tied to no alliance – a military base for no other country.

These are the essentials of any final settlement.

We will never be second in the search for such a peaceful settlement in Viet-Nam.

There may be many ways to this kind of peace: in discussion or negotiation with the governments concerned; in large groups or in small ones; in the reaffirmation of old agreements of their strenthening wih new ones.

We have stated this position over and over again, fifty times and more, to friend and foe alike. And we remain ready, with this purpose, for unconditional discussions.

These countries of southeast Asia are homes for millions of impoverished people. Each day these people rise at dawn and struggle through until the night to wrestle existence from the soil. They are often wracked by disease, plagued by hunger, and death comes at the early age of 40. ...

For our part I will ask the Congress to join in a billion dollar American investment in this effort as soon as it is underway. ...

The task is nothing less than to enrich the hopes and the existence of more than a hundred million people. And there is much to be done.

The vast Mekong River can provide food and water and power on a scale to dwarf even our own TVA. ...

*Public Papers of the Presidents of the United States: Lyndon B. Johnson, 1965*, Washington, DC: Government Printing Office, 1966, pp. 394–7.

## DOCUMENT 20   THE DRV POSITION, APRIL 1965

*North Vietnamese premier Pham Van Dong outlines a four-point settlement in a speech to the national assembly in Hanoi, 8 April 1965.*

Pham Van Dong, Premier of the Democratic Republic of Viet-Nam, elucidated the unswerving stand of the government of the D.R.V. on the Viet-Nam question in his report on government work at the second session of the United National Assembly. ...

Premier Pham Van Dong said that it is the unswerving policy of the government of the D.R.V. to strictly respect the 1954 Geneva Agreements on Viet-Nam and to correctly implement their basic provisions as embodied in the following points:

1. Recognition of the basic national rights of the Vietnamese people – peace, independence, sovereignty, unity and territorial integrity. According to the Geneva Agreements, the United States government must withdraw from South Viet-Nam United States troops, military personnel, and weapons of all kinds, dismantle all United States military bases there, cancel its 'military alliance' with South Viet-Nam. It must end its policy of intervention and aggression in South Viet-Nam. According to the Geneva Agreements, the United States government must stop its acts of war against North Viet-Nam, completely cease all encroachments on the territory and sovereignty of the D.R.V.

2. Pending the peaceful reunification of Viet-Nam, while Viet-Nam is still temporarily divided into two zones, the military provisions of the 1954 Geneva Agreements on Viet-Nam must be strictly respected. The two zones must refrain from joining any military alliance with foreign countries. There must be no foreign military bases, troops, or military personnel in their respective territory.

3. The internal affairs of South Viet-Nam must be settled by the South Vietnamese people themselves, in accordance with the program of the NFLSV [the Vietcong] without any foreign interference.

4. The peaceful reunification of Viet-Nam is to be settled by the Vietnamese people in both zones, without any foreign interference. ...

If this basis is recognized, favorable conditions will be created for the peaceful settlement of the Viet-Nam problem, and it will be possible to consider the reconvening of an international conference along the pattern of the 1954 Geneva Conference on Viet-Nam.

The government of the D.R.V. declares that any approach contrary to the above-mentioned stand is inappropriate. Any approach tending to secure a United Nations intervention in the Viet-Nam situation is also inappropriate because such approaches are basically at variance with the 1954 Geneva Agreements on Viet-Nam.

*New York Times*, 14 April 1965.

## DOCUMENT 21   LE DUAN VOWS DETERMINATION, JULY 1965

*Le Duan, the General Secretary of the Vietnamese Workers' Party, contemplates a major confrontation with the United States, in a speech to a cadre conference, 6–8 July 1965.*

[T]he U.S. is still strong enough to enter into a limited war in Vietnam, by sending ... 300,000–400,000 troops to South Vietnam. But if it switches to limited war, the U.S. still will have weaknesses which it cannot overcome. The U.S. rear area is very far away, and American soldiers are 'soldiers in chains,' who cannot fight like the French, cannot stand the weather conditions, and don't know the battlefield. ... If the U.S. puts 300–400,000 troops into the South, it will have stripped away the face of its neocolonial policy and revealed the face of an old style colonial invader. ... Thus, the U.S. will not be able to maintain its power with regard to influential sectors of the United States. If the U.S. itself directly enters the war in the South it will have to fight for a prolonged period with the people's army of the South, with the full assistance of the North and of the Socialist bloc. To fight for a prolonged period is a weakness of U.S. imperialism. The Southern revolution can fight a protracted war, while the U.S. can't, because American military, economic and political resources must be distributed throughout the world. ...

With regard to the North, the U.S. still carries out its war of distruction [*sic*], primarily by its air force: Besides bombing military targets, bridges and roads to obstruct transport and communications, the U.S. could also indiscriminately bomb economic targets, markets [,] villages, schools, hospitals, dikes, etc., in order to created confusion and agitation among the people. ... The North will not flinch for a moment before the destructive acts of the U.S. which could grow increasingly made [mad] with every passing day. The North will not count the cost. ...

If the U.S. is still more adventurous and brings U.S. and puppet troops of all their vassal states to attack the North, broadening it into a direct war in the entire country, the situation will then be different. Then it will not be we alone who still fight the U.S. but our entire camp. First the U.S. will not only be doing battle with 17 million people in the North but will also have to battle with hundreds of millions of Chinese people. ... [The DRV and China] would resist together. Could the American imperialists suppress hundreds of millions of people? Certainly they could not. If they reach a stage of desperation, would the U.S. use the atomic bomb? Our camp also has the atomic bomb. The Soviet Union has sufficient atomic strength to oppose any imperialists who wish to use the atomic bomb in order to attack a socialist country, and threaten mankind. If U.S. imperialism uses the atomic bomb in those circumstances they would be committing suicide. The

American people themselves would be the ones to stand up and smash the U.S. government when that government used atomic bombs. Would the U.S. dare to provoke war between the two blocks [*sic*] because of the Vietnam problem; would it provoke a third world war in order to put an early end to the history of U.S. imperialism and of the entire imperialist system in general[?] Would other imperialist countries, factions in the U.S. and particularly the American people, agree to the U.S. warmongers throwing them into suicide? Certainly, the U.S. could not carry out their intention, because U.S. imperialism is in a weak position and not in a position of strength.

Gareth Porter, ed., *Vietnam: The Definitive Documentation of Human Decisions*, 2 vols, Stanfordville, NY: E.M. Coleman, 1979, II, pp. 383–5.

DOCUMENT 22    CLIFFORD OPPOSES A MAJOR WAR, JULY 1965

*Clark Clifford, a senior statesman in the Democratic party, expresses opposition to escalation in a meeting with Johnson at Camp David, 25 July 1965.*

Don't believe we can win in SVN. If we send in 100,000 more, the NVN will meet us. If the NVN run out of men, the Chinese will send in volunteers. Russia and China don't intend for us to win the war. If we don't win, it is a catastrophe. If we lose 50,000+ it will ruin us. Five years, billions of dollars, 50,000 men, it is not for us.

At end of monsoon, quietly probe and search out with other countries – by moderating our position – to allow us to get out. Can't see anything but catastrophe for my country. ...

Johnson Library, box I, Meeting Notes File, Johnson Papers, Austin, TX.

# WHO'S WHO

## THE VIETNAMESE

*Bao Dai*  Last emperor of Vietnam, who first ascended to throne in 1932. Returned from exile to rule as chief of state under the French from 1949 to 1955, when Ngo Dinh Diem defeated him in a referendum.

*Duong Van Minh*  Senior army officer who led the coup against Diem in 1963, and was himself ousted in a coup in late January 1964. Took over GVN in spring 1975 and surrendered to the Communists.

*Ho Chi Minh*  Founder of the Indochinese Communist Party and creator of the Vietminh. Proclaimed Vietnam's independence from France in 1945, then fought the French for the next nine years. President of the DRV from 1945 until his death in 1969.

*Le Duan*  General secretary of the Vietnamese Workers' Party (Lao Dong), and later succeeded Ho Chi Minh as the most powerful figure in Vietnam.

*Ngo Dinh Diem*  Anti-Communist nationalist who became prime minister to Bao Dai in 1954. Ousted Bao Dai in a referendum the next year, and governed South Vietnam until being overthrown and killed in November 1963.

*Ngo Dinh Nhu*  Diem's younger brother and an influential figure in the regime, particularly in the final years. Assassinated along with Diem in 1963.

*Nguyen Cao Ky*  Prime minister of South Vietnam from 1965 to 1967, and its figurehead vice-president until 1971.

*Nguyen Khanh*  South Vietnamese general who assumed power in a bloodless coup in January 1964. Initially worked closely with the Americans, but over time fell out of favor with them. Lasted as prime minister for about a year.

*Pham Van Dong*  One of the founders of the Indochinese Communist Party, he led Vietminh delegation at the 1954 Geneva Conference. Served as the DRV's prime minister from 1950 onward, retaining that post even after reunification in 1975.

*Vo Nguyen Giap*  Close associate of Ho Chi Minh and creator of the Vietminh military organization that defeated the French and withstood the military might of the United States. As such, the chief DRV strategist from 1946 to 1975.

## THE FRENCH

*de Gaulle, Charles*  President of France after World War II and again from 1958 to 1969. Sought to reclaim Indochina for France in 1945, but in later years grew disillusioned with the war. Voiced strong opposition to American involvement in Vietnam in the 1960s.

*de Lattre de Tassigny, Jean*    French military and civilian commander in Indochina, 1950–51. Inspired his troops to several battle victories, but these were short-lived. Died of cancer in 1952.

*Mendès France, Pierre*    Politician who became an outspoken opponent of the war in Indochina. Became prime minister in June 1954 during the Geneva Conference and succeeded in securing an armistice there.

*Navarre, Henri*    Commander of French forces in Indochina, responsible for the decision to fight at Dien Bien Phu.

*Sainteny, Jean*    Banker and diplomat, sent to Vietnam in 1945 to negotiate on behalf of France with Ho Chi Minh. Would later help arrange the secret talks that led to the 1973 Paris Peace Agreement.


## THE AMERICANS

*Ball, George*    Undersecretary of state, and an early opponent of an Americanized war.

*Bowles, Chester*    Preceded Ball as undersecretary. Like Ball, he opposed making a major commitment to South Vietnam.

*Bundy, McGeorge*    Harvard dean who became national security adviser under Kennedy. Kept the post under Johnson until 1966. One of the architects of the 1965 escalation.

*Bundy, William P.*    Older brother of McGeorge, served as assistant secretary of state for far eastern affairs. Chaired the NSC Working Group that in November–December 1964 laid the groundwork for a major US escalation of the war.

*Dulles, John Foster*    Secretary of state, 1953–59, who favored full support of the French in Indochina. After 1954, he sought to build up a non-communist bastion in South Vietnam.

*Eisenhower, Dwight*    President, 1953–61. Declined to intervene militarily to relieve the French garrison at Dien Bien Phu, but supported French war effort and fully backed Diem after 1955.

*Fulbright, J. William*    Senator who chaired the Foreign Relations Committee. Shepherded the Tonkin Gulf Resolution through Congress, despite misgivings about the war. Soon turned against the escalation.

*Harkins, Paul*    Head of the Military Assistance Command, Vietnam. Famous for insisting on favorable reports from his officers.

*Harriman, W. Averell*    State Department official who represented the United States at the Geneva Conference on Laos. Instrumental in authorizing American support for the overthrow of Diem.

*Hilsman, Roger*    State Department official who played important role in promoting the coup against Diem.

*Humphrey, Hubert H.*    Vice-president under Johnson after January 1965. Had deep misgivings about Americanizing the war. Lost to Richard Nixon in the 1968 election.

*Johnson, Lyndon B.* Senator from Texas, 1949 until 1961, when he became JFK's vice-president. Succeeded Kennedy as president, and oversaw the Americanization of the war. Declined to seek re-election in 1968.

*Kennedy, John F.* President, 1961–63. US involvement deepened dramatically on his watch. Assassinated in November 1963, three weeks after the murder of Diem.

*Lansdale, Edward* Key American adviser to Ngo Dinh Diem in 1955.

*Lodge, Henry Cabot* Former senator from Massachusetts who served as ambassador to South Vietnam in 1963–64 and 1965–67. Played a key role in the coup against Diem.

*McNamara, Robert* Secretary of defense under Kennedy and Johnson, and a major architect of US policy. Became disenchanted with the war and resigned his post in 1968.

*Mansfield, Mike* Senate majority leader and former professor of Asian history. An early supporter of Diem, he eventually became opposed to a major US intervention in the war.

*Roosevelt, Franklin D.* President from 1933 until his death in 1945. Held low opinion of French colonialism, and initially favored independence for Vietnam. But had begun to soften his opposition to a French return to Indochina when he died.

*Rusk, Dean* Secretary of state under Kennedy and Johnson, and a strong proponent of a staunch US commitment to defend South Vietnam. Rejected early negotiations, and called on Hanoi and Beijing to 'leave their neighbors alone.'

*Taylor, Maxwell* Chairman of the Joint Chiefs of Staff from 1962 to 1964 and ambassador to South Vietnam in 1964–65. Recommended deeper involvement in Vietnam in 1961 as an adviser to Kennedy.

*Truman, Harry S.* As president from 1945 to 1953, took the first important step toward US involvement in Vietnam by backing the French war effort. Did not share his predecessor Franklin Roosevelt's visceral dislike of French colonialism.

*Westmoreland, William* Appointed head of military advisory mission in 1964, and would command US combat forces in the war until his departure in 1968.


OTHERS

*Kosygin, Alexei* Soviet prime minister from 1964 until his death in 1980. Visited Hanoi in February 1965 at the time of the Pleiku attack and American retaliatory bombing.

*Mao Zedong* Chinese Communist Party chairman.

*Souvanna Phouma* Prince who became prime minister of Laos in 1962 following the Geneva Conference. Held the post until Communist take-over in 1975.

*Seaborn, J. Blair* Canadian representative to the International Control Commission who paid diplomatic visits to Hanoi in the months prior to Americanization.

*Sihanouk, Norodom*    Enthroned as king of Cambodia by the French in 1941. Later abdicated, but returned as leader and worked tirelessly to preserve Cambodia's neutrality. Overthrown in March 1970.

*U Thant*    United Nations secretary general, and a native of Burma. Worked unsuccessfully to bring about a negotiated settlement of the war in the mid-1960s.

*Wilson, Harold*    Prime minister of Great Britain, 1964–70 and 1974–76. Counseled Johnson against a major escalation of the war.

*Zhou Enlai*    Foreign minister of the People's Republic of China. Played important role in 1954 Geneva Conference.

# BIBLIOGRAPHY

1   Anderson, David L. *Trapped by Success: The Eisenhower Administration and Vietnam.* New York, 1991.

2   Ashby, LeRoy and Rod Gramer. *Fighting the Odds: The Life of Senator Frank Church.* Pullman, WA, 1994.

3   Austin, Anthony. *The President's War.* Philadelphia, 1971.

4   Ball, George W. *The Past Has Another Pattern: Memoirs.* New York, 1982.

5   Baritz, Loren. *Backfire: A History of How American Culture Led Us into Vietnam and Made Us Fight the Way We Did.* New York, 1985.

6   Barnet, Richard J. *The Alliance: America, Europe, Japan: Makers of the Postwar World.* New York, 1983.

7   Barnet, Richard J. *Roots of War: The Men and Institutions Behind U.S. Foreign Policy.* New York, 1972.

8   Barrett, David M. *Uncertain Warriors: Lyndon Johnson and His Vietnam Advisers.* Lawrence, KS, 1993.

9   Bergerud, Eric M. *The Dynamics of Defeat: The Vietnam War in Hau Nghia Province.* Boulder, CO, 1991.

10  Berman, Larry. 'NSAM 263 and NSAM 273: Manipulating History.' In *Vietnam: The Early Years,* ed. Lloyd C. Gardner and Ted Gittinger. Austin, TX, 1997.

11  Berman, Larry. *Planning a Tragedy: The Americanization of the War in Vietnam.* New York, 1982.

12  Berman, William C. *William Fulbright and the Vietnam War: The Dissent of a Political Realist.* Kent, OH, 1988.

13  Beschloss, Michael R. *The Crisis Years: Kennedy and Khrushchev, 1960–1963.* New York, 1991.

14  Beschloss, Michael R. *Taking Charge: The Johnson White House Tapes, 1963–1964.* New York, 1998.

15  Billings-Yun, Melanie. *Decision Against War: Eisenhower and Dien Bien Phu, 1954.* New York, 1988.

16  Bird, Kai. *The Color of Truth: McGeorge and William Bundy, Brothers in Arms.* New York, 1988.

17  Blackburn, Robert M. *Mercenaries and Lyndon Johnson's 'More Flags': The Hiring of Korean, Filipino, and Thai Soldiers in the Vietnam War.* Jefferson, NC, 1994.

18  Blair, Anne E. *Lodge in Vietnam: A Patriot Abroad.* New Haven, CT, 1995.

19  Blum, Robert. *Drawing the Line: The Origin of American Containment Policy in East Asia.* New York, 1982.

20  Bradley, Mark Philip. *Imagining Vietnam and America: The Making of a Postcolonial Vietnam.* Chapel Hill, NC, 2000.

21  Brigham, Robert K. *Guerrilla Diplomacy: The NLF's Foreign Relations and the Vietnam War.* Ithaca, NY, 1999.
22  Brodie, Bernard. *War and Politics.* New York, 1973.
23  Burke, John P. and Fred I. Greenstein. *How Presidents Test Reality: Decisions on Vietnam, 1954 and 1965.* New York, 1989.
24  Buttinger, Joseph. *Vietnam: A Political History.* New York, 1968.
25  Buzzanco, Robert. *Masters of War: Military Dissent in the Vietnam Era.* New York, 1995.
26  Cable, James E. *The Geneva Conference of 1954 on Indochina.* New York, 1986.
27  Caro, Robert A. *The Years of Lyndon Johnson, Vol. 1, The Path to Power.* New York, 1982.
28  Chafe, William H. *The Unfinished Journey: America Since World War II,* 3rd edn. New York, 1991.
29  Chen Jian. 'China's Involvement in the Vietnam War, 1964–1969,' *China Quarterly* 142 (June 1995).
30  Clifford, Clark. *Counsel to the President: A Memoir.* New York, 1991.
31  Clodfelter, Mark. *The Limits of Airpower: The American Bombing of North Vietnam.* New York, 1989.
32  Cohen, Warren I. *Dean Rusk.* Totowa, 1980.
33  Cohen, Warren I. and Nancy Bernkopf Tucker, eds. *Lyndon Johnson Confronts the World: American Foreign Policy, 1963–1968.* New York, 1994.
34  Combs, Arthur. 'The Path Not Taken: The British Alternative to U.S. Policy in Vietnam, 1954–1956,' *Diplomatic History* 19 (Winter 1995).
35  Conkin, Paul K. *Big Daddy from the Pedernales: Lyndon Baines Johnson.* Boston, 1986.
36  Cooper, Chester. *The Lost Crusade: America in Vietnam.* New York, 1970.
37  Costigliola, Frank. *France and the United States: The Cold Alliance Since World War II.* New York, 1992.
38  Couve de Murville, Maurice. *Une politique étrangere, 1958–1969.* Paris, 1971.
39  Currey, Cecil B. *Edward Lansdale: The Unquiet American.* New York, 1988.
40  Dallek, Robert. *Flawed Giant: Lyndon Johnson and His Times, 1961–1973.* New York, 1998.
41  Dallek, Robert. 'Lyndon Johnson and Vietnam: The Making of a Tragedy,' *Diplomatic History* 20 (Spring 1996).
42  DeBenedetti, Charles. *An American Ordeal: The Antiwar Movement of the Vietnam Era.* Syracuse, NY, 1990.
43  De Silva, Peer. *Sub rosa: The CIA and the Uses of Intelligence.* New York, 1978.
44  Devillers, Philippe. *Histoire du Viet-Nam de 1940 à 1952.* Paris, 1952.
45  DiLeo, David. *George Ball, Vietnam, and the Rethinking of Containment.* Chapel Hill, 1991.
46  Dimbleby, David and David Reynolds. *An Ocean Apart: The Relationship Between Britain and America in the Twentieth Century.* New York, 1988.
47  Divine, Robert. 'Vietnam: An Episode in the Cold War.' In *Vietnam: The Early Years,* ed. Lloyd C. Gardner and Ted Gittinger. Austin, TX, 1997.
48  Dobrynin, Anatoly F. *In Confidence: Moscow's Ambassador to America's Six Cold War Presidents, 1962–1986.* New York, 1995.

49  Don, Tran Van. *Our Endless War: Inside South Vietnam.* San Rafael, CA, 1978.

50  Dugger, Ronnie. *The Politician: The Life and Times of Lyndon Johnson.* New York, 1982.

51  Duiker, William. *Ho Chi Minh.* New York, 2000.

52  Duiker, William. *The Rise of Nationalism in Vietnam, 1900–1941.* Ithaca, NY, 1976.

53  Duiker, William. *Sacred War: Nationalism and Revolution in a Divided Vietnam.* New York, 1995.

54  Duiker, William. *U.S. Containment Policy and the Conflict in Indochina.* Stanford, CA, 1994.

55  Edwards, P.G. *Crises and Commitments: The Politics and Diplomacy of Australia's Involvement in Southeast Asian Conflicts, 1948–1965.* North Sydney, Australia, 1992.

56  Ellsberg, Daniel. *Papers on the War.* New York, 1972.

57  English, John. *The Wordly Years: The Life of Lester Pearson, Vol. II, 1949–1972.* Toronto, 1992.

58  Evans, Rowland and Robert Novak. *Lyndon Johnson: The Exercise of Power.* New York, 1966.

59  Fall, Bernard. *Hell in a Very Small Place: The Siege of Dien Bien Phu.* Philadelphia, 1967.

60  Fall, Bernard. *Street Without Joy.* Harrisburg, PA., 1964.

61  Fall, Bernard. *The Two Vietnams: A Political and Military Analysis.* New York, 1967.

62  Fall, Bernard. *Viet-Nam Witness.* New York, 1964.

63  FitzGerald, Frances. *Fire in the Lake: The Vietnamese and the Americans in Vietnam.* Boston, 1972.

64  FitzSimons, Louise. *The Kennedy Doctrine.* New York, 1972.

65  Gaddis, John Lewis. *Strategies of Containment: A Critical Appraisal of Postwar American National Security Policy.* New York, 1982.

66  Gaiduk, Ilya V. *The Soviet Union and the Vietnam War.* Chicago, 1996.

67  Galbraith, John Kenneth. *A Life in Our Times.* Boston, 1981.

68  Gallucci, Robert L. *Neither Peace nor Honor: The Politics of American Military Policy in Vietnam.* Baltimore, 1975.

69  Gardner, Lloyd C. *Approaching Vietnam: From World War II through Dienbienphu.* New York, 1988.

70  Gardner, Lloyd C. *Pay Any Price: Lyndon Johnson and the Wars for Vietnam.* Chicago, 1995.

71  Gardner, Lloyd C. and Ted Gittinger, eds. *Vietnam: The Early Decisions.* Austin, TX, 1997.

72  Gelb, Leslie and Richard K. Betts. *The Irony of Vietnam: The System Worked.* Washington, DC, 1978.

73  Georges, Alfred. *Charles de Gaulle et la guerre d'Indochine.* Paris, 1974.

74  Geyelin, Philip. *Lyndon B. Johnson and the World.* New York, 1966.

75  Gibbons, William C. *The U.S. Government and the Vietnam War: Executive and Legislative Roles and Relationships*, 3 vols. Washington, DC, 1984–1988.

76  Gittinger, Ted, ed. *The Johnson Years: A Vietnam Roundtable.* Austin, TX, 1993.

77 Goldman, Eric F. *The Tragedy of Lyndon Johnson*. New York, 1969.

78 Goodman, Allan E. *The Lost Peace: America's Search for a Negotiated Settlement of the Vietnam War*. Berkeley, CA, 1978.

79 Goodwin, Richard N. *Remembering America: A Voice from the Sixties*. Boston, 1988.

80 Hammond, William M. *Public Affairs: The Military and the Media, 1962–1968*. Washington, 1988.

81 Halberstam, David. *The Best and the Brightest*. New York, 1972.

82 Halberstam, David. *Ho*. New York, 1971.

83 Hallin, Daniel C. *The 'Uncensored War': The Media and Vietnam*. New York, 1986.

84 Hammer, Ellen. *A Death in November: America in Vietnam, 1963*. New York, 1987.

85 Hammer, Ellen. *The Struggle for Indochina, 1940–1954*. Stanford, CA, 1954.

86 Harrison, James P. *The Endless War: Vietnam's Struggle for Independence*. New York, 1989.

87 Havens, Thomas R. H. *Fire Across the Sea: The Vietnam War and Japan, 1965–1975*. Princeton, NJ, 1987.

88 Heifetz, Ronald A. *Leadership Without Easy Answers*. Cambridge, MA, 1994.

89 Heinrichs, Waldo. 'Lyndon Johnson: Change and Continuity.' In *Lyndon Johnson Confronts the World: American Foreign Policy, 1963–1968*, ed. Warren I. Cohen and Nancy Bernkopf Tucker. New York, 1994.

90 Hendrickson, Paul. *The Living and the Dead: Robert McNamara and Five Lives of a Lost War*. New York, 1996.

91 Herring, George C. *America's Longest War: The United States and Vietnam, 1950–1975*, 3rd edn. New York, 1996.

92 Herring, George C., ed. *The Secret Diplomacy of the Vietnam War: The Negotiating Volumes of the Pentagon Papers*. Austin, TX, 1983.

93 Hess, Gary R. *The United States' Emergence as a Southeast Asia Power*. New York, 1987.

94 Hess, Gary R. *Vietnam and the United States: Origins and Legacy of War*, rev. edn. New York, 1998.

95 Hilsman, Roger *To Move a Nation: The Politics of Foreign Policy in the Administration of John F. Kennedy*. New York, 1967.

96 Horne, Alistair. *Harold Macmillan, Vol. II, 1957–1986*. New York, 1989.

97 Humphrey, Hubert H. *The Education of a Public Man: My Life and Politics*. Garden City, NY, 1976.

98 Hunt, Michael H. *Lyndon Johnson's War: America's Cold War Crusade in Vietnam, 1945–1968*. New York, 1996.

99 Huynh Kim Khanh. *Vietnamese Communism, 1925–1945*. New York, 1982.

100 Immerman, Richard. 'The United States and the Geneva Conference of 1954: A New Look,' *Diplomatic History* 14: 1 (Winter 1990).

101 Isaacson, Walter, and Evan Thomas. *The Wise Men: Six Friends and the World They Made: Acheson, Bohlen, Harriman, Kennan, Lovett, McCloy*. New York, 1986.

102 Jamieson, Neil L. *Understanding Vietnam*. Berkeley, 1993.

103    Janis, Irving L. *Victims of Groupthink: A Psychological Study of Foreign-Policy Decisions and Fiascoes.* Boston, 1972.

104    Jervis, Robert. *Perception and Misperception in International Politics.* Princeton, NJ, 1976.

105    Johnson, Lyndon B. *The Vantage Point: Perspectives of the Presidency, 1963–1968.* New York, 1971.

106    Joyaux, François, *La Chine et le règlement du premier conflit d'Indochine* (Genève 1954). Paris, 1979.

107    Kahin, George McT. *Intervention: How America Became Involved in Vietnam.* New York, 1987.

108    Karnow, Stanley. *Vietnam: A History.* New York, 1983.

109    Kattenburg, Paul. *The Vietnam Trauma in American Foreign Policy.* New Brunswick, NJ, 1980.

110    Kearns, Doris. *Lyndon Johnson and the American Dream.* New York, 1976.

111    Kissinger, Henry. *Diplomacy.* New York, 1994.

112    Kolko, Gabriel. *Anatomy of a War: Vietnam, the United States, and the Modern Historical Experience.* New York, 1985.

113    Kraslow, David and Stuart Loory. *The Secret Search for Peace in Vietnam.* New York, 1968.

114    Lacouture, Jean. *DeGaulle: Le Souverain, 1958–1969.* Paris, 1986.

115    Lacouture, Jean. *Ho Chi Minh: A Political Biography.* New York, 1968.

116    Lacouture, Jean. *Vietnam: Between Two Truces.* New York, 1966.

117    LaFeber, Walter. *The American Age.* New York, 1989.

118    Lam, Truong Buu, ed. *Patterns of Vietnamese Response to Foreign Intervention, 1858–1900.* New York, 1967.

119    Langguth, A.J. *Our Vietnam: The War, 1945–1975.* New York, 2000.

120    Lee, Steven Hugh. *Outposts of Empire: Korea, Vietnam, and the Origins of the Cold War in Asia.* Montreal, 1995.

121    Logevall, Fredrik. *Choosing War: The Lost Chance for Peace and the Escalation of War in Vietnam.* Berkeley, 1999.

122    Logevall, Fredrik. 'First Among Critics: Walter Lippmann and the Vietnam War,' *Journal of American-East Asian Relations* 4 (December 1995).

123    Logevall, Fredrik. 'Vietnam and the Question of What Might Have Been.' In *Kennedy: The New Frontier Revisited,* ed. Mark J. White. London, 1998.

124    Lomperis, Timothy J. *The War Everyone Lost and Won.* Baton Rouge, LA, 1984.

125    Maneli, Mieczyslaw. *War of the Vanquished.* New York, 1971.

126    Marr, David G. *Vietnam 1945.* Berkeley, CA, 1995

127    Marr, David G. *Vietnamese Anti-Colonialism, 1880–1925.* Berkeley, CA, 1971.

128    Marr, David G. *Vietnamese Tradition on Trial, 1920–1945.* Berkeley, CA, 1981.

129    May, Ernest. *'Lessons of the Past': The Use and Misuse of History in American Foreign Policy.* New York, 1973.

130    McMahon, Robert J. 'Credibility and World Power,' *Diplomatic History* 15 (Fall 1991).

131    McMaster, H.R. *Dereliction of Duty: Lyndon Johnson, Robert McNamara, the Joint Chiefs of Staff, and the Lies that Led to Vietnam.* New York, 1997.

132   McNamara, Robert S., with Brian VanDeMark. *In Retrospect: The Tragedy and Lessons of Vietnam*. New York, 1995.

133   Moïse, Edwin E. *Land Reform in China and Vietnam*. Chapel Hill, NC, 1983.

134   Moïse, Edwin E. *Tonkin Gulf and the Escalation of the Vietnam War*. Chapel Hill, NC, 1996.

135   Neustadt, Richard and Ernest R. May. *Thinking in Time: The Uses of History for Decision-Makers*. New York, 1986.

136   Newman, John M. *JFK and Vietnam: Deception, Intrigue, and the Struggle for Power*. New York, 1992.

137   Nolting, Frederick. *From Trust to Tragedy: The Political Memoir of Frederick Nolting, Kennedy's Ambassador to Diem's Vietnam*. New York, 1988.

138   O'Donnell, Kenneth P. and David F. Powers. *'Johnny, We Hardly Knew Ye': Memories of John Fitzgerald Kennedy*. Boston, 1972.

139   Olsen, James S. and Randy Roberts. *Where the Domino Fell: America and Vietnam, 1945–1995*, 2nd edn. New York, 1996.

140   Papp, Daniel S. *Vietnam: The View from Moscow, Peking, Washington*. Salisbury, NC, 1981.

141   Paterson, Thomas G., ed. *Kennedy's Quest for Victory: American Foreign Policy, 1961–1963*. New York, 1989.

142   Pearson, Lester B. *Mike: The Memoirs of the Right Honourable Lester B. Pearson Vol. III, 1957–1968*. Toronto, 1975.

143   Pelz, Stephen E. 'John F. Kennedy's 1961 Vietnam War Decisions,' *Journal of Strategic Studies* IV (1981).

144   *The Pentagon Papers: The Defense Department History of Decisionmaking on Vietnam,* The Senator Gravel edition, 5 vols Boston, 1971–72.

145   Peyrefitte, Alain. *C'était de Gaulle: La France reprend sa place dans le monde*. Paris, 1997.

146   Pike, Douglas. *Viet Cong: The Organization and Techniques of the National Liberation Front of South Vietnam*. Cambridge, MA, 1966.

147   Pike, Douglas. *Vietnam and the Soviet Union*. New York, 1987.

148   Podhoretz, Norman. *Why We Were in Vietnam*. New York, 1982.

149   Porter, Gareth. *A Peace Denied: The United States, Vietnam, and the Paris Agreements*. Bloomington, IN, 1975.

150   Powers, Thomas. *The War at Home: Vietnam and the American People, 1964–1968*. New York, 1973.

151   Prados, John. *The Hidden History of the Vietnam War*. Chicago, 1995.

152   *Public Papers of the Presidents of the United States: John F. Kennedy, 1963*. Washington, DC, 1964.

153   Race, Jeffrey. *War Comes to Long An: Revolutionary Conflict in a Vietnamese Province*. Berkeley, CA, 1972.

154   Randle, Robert. *Geneva 1954: The Settlement of the Indochina War*. Princeton, NJ, 1969.

155   Raskin, Marcus G. and Bernard Fall, eds. *The Vietnam Reader: Articles and Documents on American Foreign Policy and the Vietnam Crisis*. New York, 1965.

156   Reedy, George E. *Lyndon B. Johnson: A Memoir*. New York, 1982.

157   Reeves, Richard. *President Kennedy: Profile of Power*. New York, 1993.

158  Reischauer, Edwin O. *My Life Between Japan and America*. New York, 1986.

159  Ross, Douglas A. *In the Interests of Peace: Canada and Vietnam, 1954–1973*. Toronto, 1984.

160  Rossi, Mario. 'U Thant and Vietnam: The Untold Story,' *New York Review of Books* 17 (November 1966).

161  Rostow, Walt W. *The United States and the Regional Organization of Asia and the Pacific, 1965–1985*. Austin, TX, 1986.

162  Rotter, Andrew. *The Path to Vietnam: Origins of the American Commitment to Southeast Asia*. Ithaca, NY, 1987.

163  Ruscio, Alain. *Les communistes français et la guerre d'Indochine, 1944–1954*. Paris, 1985.

164  Rusk, Dean. *As I Saw It*. New York, 1989.

165  Rust, William J. *Kennedy and Vietnam*. New York, 1985.

166  Salisbury, Harrison. *Vietnam Reconsidered*. New York, 1984.

167  Schaller, Michael. *Altered States: the United States and Japan since Occupation*. New York, 1997.

168  Schandler, Herbert Y. *The Unmaking of a President: Lyndon Johnson and Vietnam*. Princeton, NJ, 1977.

169  Schell, Jonathan. *Time of Illusion*. New York, 1976.

170  Schlesinger, Arthur M., Jr. *A Thousand Days: John F. Kennedy in the White House*. Boston, 1965.

171  Schlesinger, Arthur M., Jr. *Bitter Heritage: Vietnam and American Democracy*. Boston, 1966.

172  Schoenbaum, Thomas J. *Waging Peace and War: Dean Rusk in the Truman, Kennedy, and Johnson Years*. New York, 1988.

173  Schulzinger, Robert D. *A Time for War: The United States and Vietnam, 1941–1975*. New York, 1997.

174  Shaplen, Robert. *Lost Revolution: The U.S. in Vietnam, 1946–1966*. New York, 1966.

175  Shaplen, Robert. *The Road from War: Vietnam, 1965–1971*. New York, 1970.

176  Shapley, Deborah. *Promise and Power: The Life and Times of Robert McNamara*. Boston, 1993.

177  Sheehan, Neil. *A Bright Shining Lie: John Paul Vann and America in Vietnam*. New York, 1988.

178  Shipway, Martin. *The Road to War: France and Vietnam, 1944–1947*. Providence, RI, 1996.

179  Short, Anthony. *The Origins of the Vietnam War*. London, 1989.

180  Sidey, Hugh. *A Very Personal Presidency: Lyndon Johnson in the White House*. New York, 1968.

181  Small, Melvin. *Johnson, Nixon and the Doves*. New Brunswick, NJ, 1986.

182  Smith, Ralph B. *An International History of the Vietnam War*, 3 vols. New York, 1980–91.

183  Smyser, W.R. *The Independent Vietnamese: Vietnamese Communism between Russia and China, 1956–1969*. Athens, OH, 1980.

184  Solberg, Carl. *Hubert Humphrey: A Biography*. New York, 1984.

185  Sorensen, Theodore C. *Kennedy*. New York, 1965.

186   Spector, Ronald H. *Advice and Support: The Early Years, 1941–1960.* Washington, 1983.
187   Steel, Ronald. *Pax Americana.* New York, 1967.
188   Steel, Ronald. *Walter Lippmann and the American Century.* Boston, 1980.
189   Steinberg, Blema S. *Shame and Humiliation: Presidentical Decision Making on Vietnam.* Pittsburgh, PA, 1996.
190   Stevenson, Charles A. *The End of Nowhere: American Policy toward Laos since 1954.* Boston, 1973.
191   Stone, I. F. *In a Time of Torment.* New York, 1967.
192   Summers, Harry G. *On Strategy: A Critical Analysis of the Vietnam War.* Novato, CA, 1982.
193   *Svensk Utrikespolitik, 1965.* Stockholm, 1966.
194   Tang, Truong Nhu, with David Chanoff and Doan Van Toai. *A Vietcong Memoir.* New York, 1985.
195   Taylor, Maxwell. *Swords and Plowshares.* New York, 1972.
196   Thakur, Ramesh. *Peacekeeping in Vietnam: Canada, India, Poland, and the International Commission.* Edmonton, Canada, 1984.
197   Thant, U. *View from the UN.* Garden City, NY, 1978.
198   Thayer, Carlyle. *War by Other Means: National Liberation and Revolution in Vietnam, 1954–1960.* Winchester, MA, 1989.
199   Thies, Wallace J. *When Governments Collide: Coercion and Diplomacy in the Vietnam Conflict, 1964–1968.* Berkeley, CA, 1980.
200   Thomas, Evan. *The Very Best Men: Four Who Dared: The Early Years of the CIA.* New York, 1995.
201   Thomson, James C. Jr., 'How Could Vietnam Happen?,' *Atlantic Monthly*, CCXXI, no. 4 (April 1968), 47–53.
202   Tonnesson, Stein. *The Vietnamese Revolution of 1945: Roosevelt, Ho Chi Minh, and de Gaulle in a World at War.* Newbury Park, CA, 1991.
203   Turley, William S. *The Second Indochina War: A Short Political and Military History, 1954–1975.* Boulder, CO, 1986.
204   Turner, Kathleen J. *Lyndon Johnson's Dual War: Vietnam and the Press.* Chicago, 1985.
205   U.S. Department of State. *Foreign Relations of the United States, 1961–1963 – Vietnam,* 4 vols. Washington, DC, 1988–1991.
206   U.S. Department of State. *Foreign Relations of the United States, 1964–1968 – Vietnam,* 3 vols Washington, DC, 1992–95.
207   Vaïsse, Maurice. *La grandeur: Politique étrangere du général de Gaulle, 1958–1969.* Paris, 1998.
208   Valenti, Jack. *A Very Human President.* New York, 1975.
209   VanDeMark, Brian. *Into the Quagmire: Lyndon Johnson and the Escalation of the Vietnam War.* New York, 1991.
210   Vandiver, Frank E. *Shadows of Vietnam: Lyndon Johnson's Wars.* College Station, TX, 1997.
211   Warner, Denis. *The Last Confucian.* Baltimore, 1963.
212   Werner, Jayne and Luu Doan Huynh, eds. *The Vietnam War: Vietnamese and American Perspectives.* New York, 1992.

213 Westad, Odd Arne, and Chen Jian, Stein Tonnesson, Nguyen Vu Tung, and James G. Hershberg, eds. '77 Conversations Between Chinese and Foreign Leaders on the Wars in Vietnam.' Cold War International History Project working paper, 1998.

214 Westmoreland, William. *A Soldier Reports*. New York, 1980.

215 Wicker, Tom. *JFK and LBJ: The Influence of Personality upon Politics*. New York, 1968.

216 Wilson, Harold. *The Labour Government, 1964–1970: A Personal Record*. London, 1971.

217 Winters, Francis X. *The Year of the Hare: America in Vietnam, January 25, 1963–February 15, 1964*. Athens, GA, 1997.

218 Woods, Randall J. *Fulbright: A Biography*. New York, 1995.

219 Young, Marilyn B. *The Vietnam Wars, 1945–1990*. New York, 1990.

220 Zagoria, Donald. *Vietnam Triangle: Moscow, Peking, Hanoi*. New York, 1967.

221 Zhai, Qiang. 'Beijing and the Vietnam Peace Talks, 1965–1968: New Evidence from Chinese Sources.' Cold War International History Project working paper, 1997

222 Zaroulis, Nancy and Gerald Sullivan. *Who Spoke Up? American Protest Against the War in Vietnam, 1963–1975*. New York, 1984.

# INDEX

Vietnamese/Chinese names are indexed by family name, ie. Ngo Dinh Diem.

Souvanna Phouma, 41, 112, 135
Soviet Union, 12, 37, 41–2, 80–1, 89
  and Franco-Vietminh war, 11, 15, 17–18,
    20–1
  and Geneva Conference, 27
  split with China, 51, 52, 63, 74
  view of Vietnam War, 51–2, 74, 91
Spellman, Francis Cardinal, 29, 31
Stalin, J., 11, 18, 20–1
Steel, Ronald, 78
Stevenson, Adlai, 72
Stone, Oliver, 39, 56
strategic hamlet program, 47, 48, 60, 119
Sullivan, William, 64–5

Taylor, General Maxwell D., 2, 41, 43–4,
    58, 65, 76, 80, 135
Taylor report (1961), 43–5, 46, 113–15
Thailand, 28
Thompson, Llewellyn, 79
Thompson, Robert G.K., 47
Tonkin, 7, 9, 10, 15
Tonkin Gulf crisis *see* Gulf of
  Tonkin crisis
Truman, Harry S., 14, 18, 19, 31, 32, 33,
    45, 135

U Thant, 63, 72, 73, 78, 87, 91, 136
United States
  collaboration with Vietminh in fighting
    Japanese during World War II, 13–14
  and communist threat, 25, 28, 102, 107
  Containment policy, 25
  'credibility' explanation for involvement in
    war, 3, 46–7
  effect of Vietnam War, 85
  elections (1964), 68, 69, 90
  escalation of commitment to war, 1–2, 69,
    70–1, 75–6, 76–7, 79–80, 81, 88,
    89–91, 92
  financial and military assistance to South
    Vietnam, 28, 29–30, 33, 35
  and Franco-Vietminh War, 14–15, 17–18,
    19, 20, 21–2, 28, 33, 86, 101
  friction with French, 30
  and Geneva Conference/Accords, 25,
    26–7, 27–8, 31
  growing isolation over policy in Vietnam
    and lack of support from Western allied
    powers, 31, 62–3, 64–5, 71–2, 87
  opposition to negotiated settlement, 44–5,
    48, 53, 54–6, 61, 72–4, 75, 77, 87–8,
    91, 92

  and overthrow of Diem government, 39,
    55–6, 86, 116–17
  reasons for involvement, 2–3
  sending of ground troops *see* ground
    troops
  support of Diem and concerns over,
    29–30, 32, 33, 42

Vance, Cyrus, 1
Vann, Lt. Col John Paul, 49
Vietcong
  attack on Pleiku, 1
  and battle at Ap Bac, 49
  and strategic hamlet program, 47
  successes and progress made, 43, 60, 68,
    69–70, 80–1, 119
  support from North Vietnam, 62
Vietminh
  and August Revolution, 13, 14
  forming of Provisional Government of
    the Democratic Republic of Vietnam,
    13
  founding of, 12–13, 95–6
  and Geneva Conference/Accords, 26, 27
  war with France *see* Franco-Vietminh
    War
Vietnam
  creation of rival government to Ho Chi
    Minh by France, 16–17
  declaration of independence by Ho Chi
    Minh (1945), 13–14, 96–8
  division into three separate regions by
    France, 7, 9
  temporary partition of by Geneva
    Accords, 26–7
Vietnam–America Friendship Association,
    14
Vietnamese nationalist movement, 9, 11
Vietnamese Nationalist Party (VNQDD),
    10
Vietnamese Workers' Party (Lao Dong), 35,
    38, 61–2, 86, 131
Vo Nguyen Giap, 13, 16, 19, 21, 36, 102–3,
    133

Warner, F.A., 52
*Washington Post*, 87
Westmoreland, General William, 2, 80–3,
    135
Wilson, Harold, 71, 136
Wilson, Woodrow, 11

Zhou Enlai, 20, 25, 27, 136

# SEMINAR STUDIES IN HISTORY

General Editors: Clive Emsley & Gordon Martel

The series was founded by Patrick Richardson in 1966. Between 1980 and 1996 Roger Lockyer edited the series before handing over to Clive Emsley (Professor of History at the Open University) and Gordon Martel (Professor of International History at the University of Northern British Columbia, Canada and Senior Research Fellow at De Montfort University).

## MEDIEVAL ENGLAND

The Pre-Reformation Church in England 1400–1530 (Second edition)
*Christopher Harper-Bill*                                                         0 582 28989 0

Lancastrians and Yorkists: The Wars of the Roses
*David R Cook*                                                                    0 582 35384 X

## TUDOR ENGLAND

Henry VII (Third edition)
*Roger Lockyer & Andrew Thrush*                                                   0 582 20912 9

Henry VIII (Second edition)
*M D Palmer*                                                                      0 582 35437 4

Tudor Rebellions (Fourth edition)
*Anthony Fletcher & Diarmaid MacCulloch*                                          0 582 28990 4

The Reign of Mary I (Second edition)
*Robert Tittler*                                                                  0 582 06107 5

Early Tudor Parliaments 1485–1558
*Michael A R Graves*                                                              0 582 03497 3

The English Reformation 1530–1570
*W J Sheils*                                                                      0 582 35398 X

Elizabethan Parliaments 1559–1601 (Second edition)
*Michael A R Graves*                                                              0 582 29196 8

England and Europe 1485–1603 (Second edition)
*Susan Doran*                                                                     0 582 28991 2

The Church of England 1570–1640
*Andrew Foster*                                                                   0 582 35574 5

## STUART BRITAIN

Social Change and Continuity: England 1550–1750 (Second edition)
*Barry Coward*                                                    0 582 29442 8

James I (Second edition)
*S J Houston*                                                     0 582 20911 0

The English Civil War 1640–1649
*Martyn Bennett*                                                  0 582 35392 0

Charles I, 1625–1640
*Brian Quintrell*                                                0 582 00354 7

The English Republic 1649–1660 (Second edition)
*Toby Barnard*                                                    0 582 08003 7

Radical Puritans in England 1550–1660
*R J Acheson*                                                     0 582 35515 X

The Restoration and the England of Charles II (Second edition)
*John Miller*                                                     0 582 29223 9

The Glorious Revolution (Second edition)
*John Miller*                                                     0 582 29222 0


## EARLY MODERN EUROPE

The Renaissance (Second edition)
*Alison Brown*                                                    0 582 30781 3

The Emperor Charles V
*Martyn Rady*                                                     0 582 35475 7

French Renaissance Monarchy: Francis I and Henry II (Second edition)
*Robert Knecht*                                                   0 582 28707 3

The Protestant Reformation in Europe
*Andrew Johnston*                                                 0 582 07020 1

The French Wars of Religion 1559–1598 (Second edition)
*Robert Knecht*                                                   0 582 28533 X

Phillip II
*Geoffrey Woodward*                                               0 582 07232 8

The Thirty Years' War
*Peter Limm*                                                      0 582 35373 4

Louis XIV
*Peter Campbell*                                                  0 582 01770 X

Spain in the Seventeenth Century
*Graham Darby*                                                    0 582 07234 4

Peter the Great
*William Marshall*                                                0 582 00355 5

## EUROPE 1789–1918

Britain and the French Revolution
*Clive Emsley*                                                    0 582 36961 4

Revolution and Terror in France 1789–1795 (Second edition)
*D G Wright*                                                      0 582 00379 2

Napoleon and Europe
*D G Wright*                                                      0 582 35457 9

Nineteenth-Century Russia: Opposition to Autocracy
*Derek Offord*                                                    0 582 35767 5

The Constitutional Monarchy in France 1814–48
*Pamela Pilbeam*                                                  0 582 31210 8

The 1848 Revolutions (Second edition)
*Peter Jones*                                                     0 582 06106 7

The Italian Risorgimento
*M Clark*                                                         0 582 00353 9

Bismark & Germany 1862–1890 (Second edition)
*D G Williamson*                                                  0 582 29321 9

Imperial Germany 1890–1918
*Ian Porter, Ian Armour and Roger Lockyer*                        0 582 03496 5

The Dissolution of the Austro-Hungarian Empire 1867–1918 (Second edition)
*John W Mason*                                                    0 582 29466 5

Second Empire and Commune: France 1848–1871 (Second edition)
*William H C Smith*                                               0 582 28705 7

France 1870–1914 (Second edition)
*Robert Gildea*                                                   0 582 29221 2

The Scramble for Africa  (Second edition)
*M E Chamberlain*                                                 0 582 36881 2

Late Imperial Russia 1890–1917
*John F Hutchinson*                                               0 582 32721 0

The First World War
*Stuart Robson*                                                   0 582 31556 5


## EUROPE SINCE 1918

The Russian Revolution (Second edition)
*Anthony Wood*                                                    0 582 35559 1

Lenin's Revolution: Russia, 1917–1921
*David Marples*                                                   0 582 31917 X

Stalin and Stalinism (Second edition)
*Martin McCauley*                                                 0 582 27658 6

The Weimar Republic (Second edition)
*John Hiden*                                                    0 582 28706 5

The Inter-War Crisis 1919–1939
*Richard Overy*                                                 0 582 35379 3

Fascism and the Right in Europe, 1919–1945
*Martin Blinkhorn*                                             0 582 07021 X

Spain's Civil War (Second edition)
*Harry Browne*                                                  0 582 28988 2

The Third Reich (Second edition)
*D G Williamson*                                               0 582 20914 5

The Origins of the Second World War (Second edition)
*R J Overy*                                                     0 582 29085 6

The Second World War in Europe
*Paul MacKenzie*                                               0 582 32692 3

Anti-Semitism before the Holocaust
*Albert S Lindemann*                                           0 582 36964 9

The Holocaust: The Third Reich and the Jews
*David Engel*                                                   0 582 32720 2

Germany from Defeat to Partition, 1945–1963
*D G Williamson*                                               0 582 29218 2

Britain and Europe since 1945
*Alex May*                                                     0 582 30778 3

Eastern Europe 1945–1969: From Stalinism to Stagnation
*Ben Fowkes*                                                    0 582 32693 1

Eastern Europe since 1970
*Bülent Gökay*                                                 0 582 32858 6

The Khrushchev Era, 1953–1964
*Martin McCauley*                                              0 582 27776 0

## NINETEENTH-CENTURY BRITAIN

Britain before the Reform Acts: Politics and Society 1815–1832
*Eric J Evans*                                                 0 582 00265 6

Parliamentary Reform in Britain c. 1770–1918
*Eric J Evans*                                                 0 582 29467 3

Democracy and Reform 1815–1885
*D G Wright*                                                   0 582 31400 3

Poverty and Poor Law Reform in Nineteenth-Century Britain, 1834–1914:
From Chadwick to Booth
*David Englander*                                              0 582 31554 9

The Birth of Industrial Britain: Economic Change, 1750–1850
*Kenneth Morgan*                                               0 582 29833 4

Chartism (Third edition)
*Edward Royle*                                                   0 582 29080 5

Peel and the Conservative Party 1830–1850
*Paul Adelman*                                                  0 582 35557 5

Gladstone, Disraeli and later Victorian Politics (Third edition)
*Paul Adelman*                                                  0 582 29322 7

Britain and Ireland: From Home Rule to Independence
*Jeremy Smith*                                                  0 582 30193 9


## TWENTIETH-CENTURY BRITAIN

The Rise of the Labour Party 1880–1945 (Third edition)
*Paul Adelman*                                                  0 582 29210 7

The Conservative Party and British Politics 1902–1951
*Stuart Ball*                                                   0 582 08002 9

The Decline of the Liberal Party 1910–1931 (Second edition)
*Paul Adelman*                                                  0 582 27733 7

The British Women's Suffrage Campaign 1866–1928
*Harold L Smith*                                                0 582 29811 3

War & Society in Britain 1899–1948
*Rex Pope*                                                      0 582 03531 7

The British Economy since 1914: A Study in Decline?
*Rex Pope*                                                      0 582 30194 7

Unemployment in Britain between the Wars
*Stephen Constantine*                                           0 582 35232 0

The Attlee Governments 1945–1951
*Kevin Jefferys*                                                0 582 06105 9

The Conservative Governments 1951–1964
*Andrew Boxer*                                                  0 582 20913 7

Britain under Thatcher
*Anthony Seldon and Daniel Collings*                            0 582 31714 2


## INTERNATIONAL HISTORY

The Eastern Question 1774–1923 (Second edition)
*A L Macfie*                                                    0 582 29195 X

The Origins of the First World War (Second edition)
*Gordon Martel*                                                 0 582 28697 2

The United States and the First World War
*Jennifer D Keene*                                              0 582 35620 2

Anti-Semitism before the Holocaust
*Albert S Lindemann*                                            0 582 36964 9

The Origins of the Cold War, 1941–1949 (Second edition)
*Martin McCauley*                                    0 582 27659 4

Russia, America and the Cold War, 1949–1991
*Martin McCauley*                                    0 582 27936 4

The Arab–Israeli Conflict
*Kirsten E Schulze*                                  0 582 31646 4

The United Nations since 1945: Peacekeeping and the Cold War
*Norrie MacQueen*                                    0 582 35673 3

Decolonisation: The British Experience since 1945
*Nicholas J White*                                   0 582 29087 2

The Origins of the Vietnam War
*Fredrik Logevall*                                   0 582 31918 8

The Vietnam War
*Mitchell Hall*                                      0 582 32859 4


## WORLD HISTORY

China in Transformation 1900–1949
*Colin Mackerras*                                    0 582 31209 4

Japan faces the World, 1925–1952
*Mary L Hanneman*                                    0 582 36898 7

Japan in Transformation, 1952–2000
*Jeff Kingston*                                      0 582 41875 5


## US HISTORY

American Abolitionists
*Stanley Harrold*                                    0 582 35738 1

The American Civil War, 1861–1865
*Reid Mitchell*                                      0 582 31973 0

America in the Progressive Era, 1890–1914
*Lewis L Gould*                                      0 582 35671 7

The United States and the First World War
*Jennifer D Keene*                                   0 582 35620 2

The Truman Years, 1945–1953
*Mark S Byrnes*                                      0 582 32904 3

The Origins of the Vietnam War
*Fredrik Logevall*                                   0 582 31918 8

The Vietnam War
*Mitchell Hall*                                      0 582 32859 4